MW01541962

Dr. Zsolt Talabér

Pigeons and their Economical Health Care

Dr. Zsolt Talabér

Pigeons and their Economical Health Care

Translated from the Hungarian by
David Robert Evans

Editor and veterinary consultant:
Botond Siklódi, D.V.M.

Cover photo:
Jama

ISBN 9781089848509

Contents

Preface

The world around us has changed dramatically in the last few decades, and this is no less true of pigeon breeding. Not so long ago, a pigeon fancier kept a little potassium permanganate at home, a little garlic extract, and a little paraffin, and this was more or less adequate to preserve the health of his flock. Those days are over. In the last few years, a number of viruses and bacteria have appeared in our environment which pigeons had previously not encountered. These new types of pathogens have caught the birds' immune system unprepared, causing high rates of illness and death in certain flocks, in wider regions, and in whole countries.

These new pathogens, or the more resistant variants of old ones, have appeared in all significant pigeon breeding areas. Thanks to easier passage over national borders, imports of birds for breeding, international races and shows, and the buying and selling of birds, newer and newer pathogens have appeared, spreading around the pigeon stocks of different countries, generating endless problems, damage, work and expenses for fanciers. A good example of this is the spread of circovirus, which has raised its ugly head in some countries' pigeon stocks; if news and hands-on evidence are to be believed, it is spreading among pigeons on a continuous basis. The circovirus attacks and damages the bird's immune system, its defence mechanism (in a similar fashion to HIV in humans), as a result of which the pigeon becomes defenceless against attack from all the other pathogens.

This book not only strives to present the most important pigeon diseases, including the newest ones, but also tries to assist in protecting the health of the flock in the most economical and successful, and not least most environmentally friendly way possible. Countless new medicines and supplements have appeared on the market in recent years, and continue to appear almost every week. These products are effective against certain ailments, but treatment is not the first step in keeping pigeon flocks healthy. On the contrary, treatment with medicines is a necessary evil (an evil because the majority of active ingredients have adverse side-effects – if nothing else, then their effect on your wallet) that we must always take great care with, as overuse of medication – as we will discuss in greater detail later – puts great strain not only on the fancier's financial resources, but on the environment, and, most of all, on the health of the pigeon itself.

The first section of the book deals with the prevention of epidemics, pigeon care hygiene, and maintaining the level of the pigeon's immune state. It describes the methods and techniques that – after a financial investment that will soon be recouped – are for the most part enough to guarantee the health of our pigeons, and thereby their highest level of performance.

The second section of the book deals with the general characteristics of medicines and supplements, and with the associated knowledge that is a necessary part of modern pigeon breeding. A significant proportion of preparations can be acquired and used without a prescription, so we should be clear about the objective and theoretical basis of each form of treatment, that is, about the way in which a preparation has its effect within the bird's body. We should know how to treat our flock with these over-the-counter (OTC) preparations, and we should also know how NOT to treat it. We must be aware of why we do what we do, we must know the principles and how they relate to practice, for this is how we can make progress, and think in terms of our flock.

In the third section, we discuss the most important contagious and non-contagious diseases in pigeons. We deal with their causes, symptoms, prevention and treatment. We consider in turn the active ingredients and methods which are currently considered to be the most effective in the many countries across the world with pigeon-fancying traditions.

The **fourth section** comprises a description of the active ingredients of medications that have been available for a longer time and those that have been developed more recently, and a guide to their use.

*

This guide is not a university textbook. It contains a variety of important information, but is no substitute for knowledge to be gained at university veterinary courses. In other words, we should regard the maintenance of the health of our flock as a task that we share with our chosen veterinary surgeon; we should ask for their collaboration, accept their advice, and follow their recommendations regarding medicines. **Economical, effective and safe treatment always begins with a precise diagnosis**, which in most instances requires veterinary expertise. Many years of experience go to show that, in the vast majority of instances, "diagnoses" produced without professional veterinary participation, and medicines acquired second-hand or at random, do much more damage to the pigeon flock than good – damage that is often irreparable.

Let there be no misunderstanding: I do not wish to underestimate the undoubted expertise of experienced pigeon fanciers, from whom, as a veterinary surgeon, I have learned a huge amount, and I know the same to be true of many of my colleagues. It appears that over the long term it is the close cooperation between fanciers and veterinary surgeons that produces the best and most successful pigeon flocks, whether we take national or international examples as our guide.

Last, but not least, I honestly hope that my fellow veterinarians active in pigeon health will find some fresh and useful information in this book.

*

As this book is available in a number of different languages and countries, we have, in addition to clarity of exposition, endeavoured to use those (specialist) terms that are most commonly used worldwide. As these are not always the same as those used in a particular locality, we appreciate the reader's patience and understanding in this.

***

Warning!

The drugs that appear in the book are generally not to be given to meat pigeons condemned for human consumption, or only under strict conditions! Most drugs can only be administered to these animals with a veterinary prescription and observing the withdrawal period as directed by the veterinary surgeon.

Dr. Zsolt Talabér

I. Maintaining good health without recourse to medicines

We are well aware that nowadays the healthcare of pigeon flocks is inconceivable without the use of medicines – whether for scheduled preventive use or for healing treatment on a case-by-case basis. Yet we continuously strive to keep the use of medicines to a minimum. This is not only in our own interest, but equally that of the pigeons, as well as their local and more general environment.

If we do not have to spend a lot on medicines, this means that our flock is healthy, but this does not happen of its own accord. The utilization of what we discuss here in the first section of the book is absolutely necessary for us **to manage the health of the flock and prevent the majority of diseases**, and, if it does prove inevitable, to provide treatment in the most effective and economic way, and with the least damage to the environment.

We have grouped the issues in this chapter into three sections:

1. Prevention of epidemics
2. Hygiene
3. The immune system and stress

This division is a trifle arbitrary, and, as we will see, there is considerable overlap between the sections, but we hope that it makes the material easier to access.

1. Prevention of epidemics

There are many ways of defining the precautions to be taken against epidemics. By 'epidemics' we mean **contagious diseases** and the way in which they **spread**, while by prevention we mean the principles and methods with the help of which **we try to protect our flock from the pathogens** that cause these diseases.

It is not an easy task. When moving from one place to another, pigeons, like all other animals, take all the bacteria, viruses, fungi and parasites in and on their bodies with them – the whole menagerie, as it were. Moreover pigeon breeding, in particular the use of racing pigeons, quite literally knows no bounds. At exhibitions, races and fairs, our pigeons not only travel a lot within their country, but often cross national borders to return to their lofts. During transportation and flying, in the course of exhibitions and fairs, coming into contact with countless other pigeons (and other birds), or at least being in the same space as them, they can catch or transmit many types of pathogens they were previously unaware of.

Such is the nature of this sport. But, precisely because of this, we must do everything we can to protect our pigeons from repeated attacks from hordes of pathogens. And this is not possible without implementing certain **measures to prevent epidemics**.

Prevention of epidemics is not only important outside the yard, i.e. during transportation on domestic and international trips and while flying. We must also maintain continuous protection within the yard, as even when at home our pigeons are exposed to the danger of infection day and night – a danger which is sometimes presented by the owner himself. Prevention of epidemics must be in place between lofts; indeed, even within the loft we must do all we can to see that pathogens are transferred from diseased to healthy birds as little as possible, or not at all.

Thus we can consider prevention of epidemics as the breaking of the chain of infection, and separate it into the following components:

- **outside the yard**
- **between the yard and the outside world**
- **between lofts**
- **within the loft**

Let us examine these in more detail. We cannot claim that each of the following recommendations can be observed for all flocks, as each yard has its own different characteristics. Certain methods can only be implemented in a particular place with considerable difficulty, and so will not be applicable. But **the more methods of prevention of epidemics you can successfully implement, the more healthy and beautiful a flock you will have in the long run**. And the beneficial effect on your wallet you will feel even more quickly.

Some of the following tips will seem banal to some, but we should immediately note that even the most experienced fanciers sometimes forget about the most basic measures to be taken against epidemics. It does no harm to look at these in turn.

Prevention of epidemics outside the yard

As we discussed above, each flock, and within that each individual pigeon has its own “menagerie”, that is to say the entirety of the bacteria, viruses, fungi, and internal and external parasites which are present in or on its body. These are for the most part innocent creatures that do not cause disease, but there can be pathogens among them, too. **One of the fundamental rules for the prevention of epidemics is that birds carrying and spreading pathogens are not to be allowed amongst healthy ones.** So we must not take a visibly ill pigeon to an exhibition, race, fair, etc., because in doing so we not only compromise our reputation, but also break the law, not to mention infecting others' flocks.

In general, we can say that most people observe this rule; the problem begins when **a seemingly healthy but actually infected pigeon** is among the healthy ones, carrying and releasing pathogens and spreading diseases among them. This can only be avoided if we pursue continuous prevention of epidemics in our flock, an integral part of which is the birds' systematic vaccination.

The situation is rather more complicated than it might first appear, however, for it is not only the meeting of the various flocks that makes travel, exhibitions and races a direct threat of infection and spread of disease. A pigeon locked in a cage and transported over a longer distance will become stressed. In the course of a lengthy or heightened state of stress, hormonal processes occur that suppress the operation of the immune system or the body's defence mechanism. (This will be discussed in detail later.) The **weakening of the body's defence mechanism** can lead to the invigoration and multiplication of pathogens (viruses, bacteria, fungi, parasites) formerly repressed and hidden in various organs. The pathogens are then released into the outside world in great quantities: a pigeon that was previously healthy becomes a dangerous, continuous and massive source of infection.

Transportation and its related tasks (putting in cages, etc.) put considerable stress on the pigeons in any case, and so every effort must be taken to see that **the vehicle used for transportation is not overcrowded**. Overcrowding not only worsens stress, but also helps the transfer of pathogens from one bird to another. Ideally, pigeons from different breeders should be transported in different vehicles, or at least in separated sections of the same vehicle. This is impossible to implement in the majority of cases, of course, and so the best we can aim for is to transport our pigeons together with flocks that are known to us, whose state of health we know to be trustworthy.

Prevention of epidemics between the yard and the outside world

When considering the prevention of epidemics between the yard and the outside world, we treat our flock and the place it is housed as a unit, and as such we try to use every available method **to keep it as isolated from the outside world as possible.**

This part of the prevention of epidemics is one of the most crucial aspects of preserving pigeons' health, as the boundary of the yard is what separates the flock from the outside world, buzzing as it is with pathogens. It is inside the yard that pigeons spend the most time, and so it is here that they are most often exposed to infection (e.g. wild birds flying in); this is the area whose boundary the fancier crosses many times each day, each time carrying in huge numbers of pathogens with him.

The yard cannot be made airtight, of course, and so in theory the wind alone can bring in pathogens, though the practical significance of this is very minimal. Visits by wild birds represent a much greater danger, as a wild pigeon, sparrow etc. flying in amidst the flock will always carry pathogens which might infect the pigeons. So the presence of wild birds must be restricted as much as possible. The lofts must be designed such that wild birds cannot fly into them. We should refrain from leaving drinkers and feeders in the yard, for these only serve to lure outsiders in, and bowls that do remain outside should be disinfected before being used again. It is clear that we cannot prevent wild birds from excreting above the area of the yard, but by putting a fence around the aviary and cleaning it regularly we can diminish the risk of infectious pathogens spreading via their droppings.

Experience shows that it is not visits by wild birds but those of **the fanciers themselves** that present the greatest risk of infection to their flocks. Fanciers may present a danger to their flocks in two ways. On the one hand, they bring large amounts of pathogens into the pigeons' yard from the outside world on their shoes, clothes and skin. On the other hand, and this represents a greater danger, **they introduce the widest variety of diseases amongst their pigeons when taking in newly-acquired specimens that are infectious and carry pathogens**. This is the subject of the following, highly significant section.

*

A special and extremely important part of the prevention of epidemics is the introduction to the flock of new pigeons acquired from elsewhere. Possibly the greatest damage in pigeon-keeping is associated with the inclusion of newly-purchased pigeons, and it is surprising how courageously the vast majority of fanciers will put their freshly acquired birds, whose state of health (or rather, of illness) is a complete mystery, among their cherished favourites. It is not rare for a flock to decline in catastrophic measure as a result of a single diseased pigeon being introduced into it, losing the best of its most beautiful specimens.

Mankind invented the **quarantine** back in medieval times, when, in the light of its importance, in many places those violating it would be punished by death. This only goes to show how significant a measure it is, one that, with a little attention, and a minimal, quickly recouped cost, can easily be implemented in our own yard.

The primary objective of the quarantine is that an infectious specimen not be allowed to be among the other pigeons. However **it is not only visibly diseased birds that are infectious; those appearing to be healthy can also spread pathogens**.

Every infectious disease has its **lag period**, the period of time, usually a few days or weeks, when the animal is already infected, but does not yet display any symptoms, that is, appears to be healthy. But, and here is the point, **it is capable of releasing**

pathogens before any symptoms of the illness appear, that is, independently from them.

Similarly, **an animal that has survived a disease** no longer displays its symptoms, but can still **release its pathogens in huge quantities**, continuing to infect its environment. Furthermore, there are pathogens – the salmonellas that cause paratyphoid are a typical example – which can remain in the pigeon's body for a long time, even a number of years, without displaying any symptoms. Such a pigeon appears to be healthy, but once in the flock it releases salmonella bacteria that our pigeons have never encountered, thus setting a real epidemic in motion.

The development and operation of the quarantine

Quarantine is only valuable if the newly-acquired pigeon, whose state of health is unknown, is **not in contact** with the other pigeons **in any way**. From this it follows that there must be no exchange of air between the quarantine and the place where the rest of the pigeons are kept; indeed, every effort should be taken to ensure that the cage or cages designated as the quarantine are kept in a separate building, or failing this in a remote part of the yard, as far from the rest of the flock as possible. We should bear in mind the direction of the wind: the dominant direction should be towards the quarantine, not away from the quarantine towards the flock.

The size of the quarantine

The capacity of the quarantine should be tailored to the flock in question, bearing in mind its size and the frequency of purchases and new admissions. Of course we should be aware of our options: the quarantine can be a separate building, but it can easily be a home-made wire cage which holds a couple of pigeons, and which we place in the corner of the yard furthest from the loft. It is not the size or "gleam" of the quarantine that matters, but how well we observe the rules associated with it.

Equipping the quarantine

The quarantine must be equipped with designated feeders and drinkers. It is a fundamental principle that things can only be brought into the quarantine, not taken out, or at least only under certain conditions, and only after being thoroughly disinfected.

As one can spread pathogens oneself (through dirt attached to shoes, clothes and the skin), systematic use of **separate clothes and especially shoes**, which are only used in or directly around the quarantine, is recommended. It is a good idea to place a tray in front of the quarantine, into which we place a large sponge previously soaked in water rich in disinfectant. This gives us a simple but effective shoe disinfectant. If we have been working in the quarantine, we should use this disinfectant upon leaving without fail, and in addition we should, of course, always wash our hands thoroughly! We should plan the day's feeding and cleaning programme, etc., such that we always deal with the healthy flock first, and **leave the inspection of the quarantine to the end of the day's duties**, after which we do not return directly to the main flock.

Period of quarantine

The lag period of diseases varies, and is usually a matter of days or weeks. No absolute value can be given for the period of quarantine, but a period of at least three or four weeks is necessary for the reliable prevention of epidemics. This can depend on a number of factors, e.g. whether our flock has been vaccinated against paramyxovirus. As the lag period of this illness can be as long as six weeks, in the case of an uninoculated and thus susceptible flock, a minimum of six weeks' quarantine is recommended.

Tasks associated with the quarantine

During the period of quarantine we observe the new specimen on a regular basis to see whether it shows any symptoms of some disease. Meanwhile we treat it for worms, which equally refers to internal and external parasites, and also brings protection against **canker** and **coccidiosis**. If the feeding of the pigeon in its previous location was very different, then during this time we **gradually** make it accustomed to the feeding mix we use.

There can also be a need for treatment with **antibiotics** during quarantine, but this must not be done as a matter of course. The best plan of action is if we request a **susceptibility test** from our veterinary surgeon. On such occasions it is best to take the sample directly from the pigeon itself (throat discharge and faeces). If this is not feasible, we should use a sterile syringe to suck a few drops out of the fresh faeces, and take this to be tested. The sample is used to grow a bacterial culture, i.e. it is spread onto a culture medium, and incubated at 37 degrees Celsius. The test not only answers the question of what kinds of pathogenic bacteria are present in the pigeon, but that of which antibiotics it is advisable to use. The advantage of the test is that in most cases it produces results quickly, within a day or two, and that, with these in hand, we do not treat the pigeon "blind", in an uninformed fashion, but with the antibiotics that will really have an effect.

During quarantine we must also strive to **stimulate the pigeon's immune system**, the technique of which will be discussed in the following sections. There may also be a need for vaccination: this should always be decided by the veterinary surgeon on a case by case basis, and it does no harm if he is aware of the pigeon's "vaccination history". These **necessary vaccinations** can lengthen the quarantine period.

After three (or more) weeks have passed, and after the necessary tests, treatments and vaccinations have been completed, we can introduce the new pigeons among the rest of the flock, taking the numbers allowed in each cage into account, of course, that is to say avoiding overcrowding. This will be the subject of the next section, entitled "Hygiene".

*

We often take pigeons out of the yard to fairs or markets, and of course almost as often bring them back, if we do not manage a sale. Birds that have been to a fair represent a danger of infection for the flock that has remained at home, and so it is advisable to keep specimens earmarked for sale that are transported frequently in a separate loft, and to move them directly from there. We should also endeavour to allow the pigeons to come into contact with other birds as little as possible within the premises of the fair.

Clearly it would be ideal if birds returning from races and fairs could be accommodated in a separate location, as they present a danger of infection for the others. In general, it would be fantastic if pigeons could be separated from one another according to their use, age, value, future activity, and so on, and be kept and moved in these different groups. The implementation of such a scheme is clearly impossible, however, as in the end we would need almost as many lofts as we have birds. And in the process we would miss the point, too: the magic, grace of pigeon racing, indeed the artistry of fancying itself. The whole affair would become self-conscious and restricted, and lose its meaning. But we should employ as many techniques of prevention of epidemics as we can, because **every single one of these measures means greater protection for our pigeons**. Let us not forget: a lot of little steps can take us closer to success, which in our case means keeping our flock healthy in an economical way and maximizing its achievement.

Prevention of epidemics between lofts

If we keep pigeons in a number of different places in a single yard, then the flocks in the various cages can **vary in terms of their state of health**. This can be a result, for example, of giving specimens that vary in their age and use different vaccinations at different times.

The epidemiological situation can also vary from loft to loft when a disease rears its ugly head in one of them. On such an occasion, we would no doubt like to stop the pathogen from being transferred to the other lofts. In this instance, we need to use essentially the same techniques as discussed above: we earmark the infected cage as the temporary “quarantine”, and operate it accordingly. If we succeed in preventing the infection from being carried to the other lofts, we can save ourselves considerable damage, and indeed a lot of money. But even if we only manage to slow down rather than stop the spread of the disease within the yard, this is better than nothing, as it gives us time actively to defend the flocks in the other lofts by preparing them against the particular illness in question.

Irrespective of this, we should strive as much as possible to maintain the immune state of every pigeon in our yard at the highest possible level, a goal that, in addition to a scheduled vaccination programme, we can principally achieve by keeping the birds in an optimal fashion. We will discuss these in more detail in the section “Hygiene”.

Prevention of epidemics within the loft

One characteristic feature of infectious diseases is that the pathogen spreads from one animal to another, gradually infecting an increasing number of specimens, causing illness in a certain proportion of them. (Here we should emphasize again, because it is so important for a number of reasons, that **not every infected animal becomes ill, that is displays the symptoms characteristic of the disease**. A specimen can remain infected for a long period, even for years, without any symptoms, that is **it appears entirely healthy, but continues to carry and spread the pathogen!**) So, if for some reason one of our pigeons is infected in some way, the pathogen, be it a virus, bacterium or parasite, will sooner or later spread within the loft, often without being noticed. Clearly, we do not want this to occur, but to stop it we must consistently provide prevention every day.

There are four key strategies **for slowing down the spread of infection within a loft**:

1. Visibly diseased birds shed the pathogens in large quantities, and so should be separated from the others and locked into a quarantine.

2. We destroy the pathogens released into the outside world or the loft by specimens that are ill or in the lag period; that is, we disinfect the yard.

3. We lessen the numbers of pathogens in a given body; in other words, we give the ill pigeons medical treatment.

4. We treat the specimens that still have hope of avoiding the disease in a preventive fashion.

Pathogens are transferred from ill birds to the outside world via various excretions, e.g. nasal excretions, tears, throat excretions, faeces, urine, etc. We can read about how to quell these dangers in the section “Hygiene”; here I would merely draw the reader’s attention to the fact that in the event of an illness, we must perform hygienic procedures, i.e. cleaning and disinfecting, regularly – **much more regularly**.

When the illness is reported, we must follow points 1, 2 and 3 at all costs, and follow point 4 depending on the nature of the pathogen. (In the case of most infectious diseases, it is recommended that all birds are treated medically, but the nature and particularly the duration of preventive treatment can be different from the medical treatment.) Naturally, both medical and preventive treatment must always be completed in a carefully considered fashion, that is, once a **precise diagnosis** has been established.

If the medical treatment is completed and the disease has “ceased” within the flock, the birds which have recovered and which no longer release pathogens may return to their original lofts. If, however, there remain pigeons after the course of treatment that have not been returned to a completely clean bill of health, it is advisable to keep them in the sick-bay a while longer, and continue **what is now individual treatment** of those specimens that are slower to recover. On the one hand, this saves us money, while on the other, we do not burden those that have recovered, and their surroundings, with unnecessary medication. Instead, we can concentrate on the treatment of the invalids, to whom, for example, we can measure out medication in practical capsules on an individual basis. Once they are returned to full health **and** they no longer release pathogens, they can also return to their original locations.

*

The importance of the prevention of epidemics cannot be overemphasized, as it can make or break the success of a whole flock. And yet, after reading this section, some will have doubts as to the effectiveness of prevention, or question whether it is feasible at all. For even if we do not take pathogens into the yard ourselves, whatever we might do to defend it from the wind or from wild birds, we cannot provide protection that is absolute; what is more, pigeons often leave the yard of their own accord. And so our flock is bound to be infected sooner or later.

This is indeed the case. Even a flock carefully isolated from the outside world will regularly become infected, perhaps more often than we might think, in exactly the ways mentioned above: the wind, wild birds, the fancier's hat, or perhaps a visitor's shoe. But it is not insignificant **how regularly** these inflows of infection occur, and, even more importantly, **how many pathogens** the various infections bring into the flock.

We can illustrate the issue by means of an example: if on a pleasant summer afternoon three wasps accidentally fly through the window of the room, we do not panic, but deal with them comfortably. The situation is quite different if there are three hundred of them. In the same way, the bodies of the pigeons can easily overcome those pathogens that appear rarely and in small quantities; indeed, these little floating pathogens are even useful in keeping the birds' immune systems in check, in an "incensed" state of readiness. However, as soon as these attacks become too regular and/or the attackers arrive in too great numbers, the situation is reversed: after a while, **the pigeon's immune system becomes worn out**, it falls ill, and begins to release the pathogens itself, in huge quantities. Then, sadly, we can say that the enemy has half-captured the castle.

*

Finally, in the light of its significance, let us summarize the fundamental principles of the prevention of epidemics. Our aim must be as follows:

A specimen that is infected or suspected of infection should not be able to be in contact either directly (e.g. shared loft) **or indirectly** (e.g. common equipment, the owner's clothes) **with the rest of the flock that is free of the pathogen**.

It is evident that in pigeon racing it is impossible to achieve absolute isolation from risks of infection, and it would be nonsense to press for it. Nevertheless, where possible, **the potential for infection and the development of the chain of infection must continuously be kept to a minimum**, and the simple truth is that this depends for the most part on the pigeon fancier himself.

2. Hygiene

There are many things we can associate with animal hygiene. In short, we can say that animal hygiene includes all the requirements we need to satisfy in order for animals to live amongst **the most optimal possible conditions** in the place they are kept, while causing as little burden to their environment as possible. These requirements include the way in which the birds are kept, ventilation, food and drink provision, and the cleanliness of the loft.

Living space - Overcrowding

Wherever we keep our pigeons, the first priority is to avoid overcrowding. **Overcrowding is the cause of countless problems**, damage which can only be dealt with temporarily and at great expense. Reaching the level of and maintaining overcrowding is **one of the surest ways of throwing away money and polluting the environment**.

All animals require a certain living space, just as humans do. If this living space falls below the necessary level, we have to face the following consequences for our pigeon flock:

- permanent, adverse stress effect appears
- the birds' use of energy and vitamin needs increase
- the oxygen level of the air decreases
- the concentration of carbon dioxide and other harmful gases in the air increases (e.g. ammonia), as does humidity
- in summer it is even warmer in the loft, while in winter everything is damp from the humidity
- the ratio of feeders and drinkers to birds is too low, and they become dirty too quickly
- it becomes uncomfortable and essentially impossible to perform necessary tasks in the loft, which only worsens the increasing level of dirt
- pathogens in the loft become more abundant
- infectious diseases spread more quickly and more easily

Overcrowding, then, leads to a degradation in the conditions of the birds' habitat, which necessarily results in a decline in performance and strength, and in illness, both for individual birds and for the flock as a whole.

Naturally, if we take the items in the above list in turn, we see that we can protect against each one, thus avoiding the degradation of the flock. We can counteract the effect of stress to some extent with an increased dosage of certain agents, we can provide extra vitamins and more feed, clean more frequently, use more disinfectant, scatter ammonia bonding substances, wash up every hour, and measure out medicines on an almost continuous basis. In a word, we generate much more work for ourselves than is necessary, our expenditures will be much higher, and we bother the birds needlessly. Overcrowding leaves no one feeling better.

We can eliminate overcrowding in two ways: we can lessen the size of the flock, or increase the space for it. In general, **three pigeons per cubic metre** is advised, and it is particularly important not to overstep this in closed lofts with poor ventilation. Even in open, well-ventilated cages, we should not keep many more birds than this. It is **at this optimal level of flock density that we can keep our pigeons in the most economical and most environmentally-friendly fashion**. This is how our flock will be as healthy as possible, and this is when we can expect the greatest performance from it. It has been proved time and time again – not only in pigeon-breeding – that investment in buildings and their extension is recouped in the medium- to long-term, and ensures economical performance and output, while **an overcrowded flock only brings continuous bother, expense and trouble**.

Air Hygiene

Air is what we can survive a lack of for the shortest time; it is oxygen that the body needs to intake the most often. So it is logical that the quality of air inhaled is a key factor in pigeon health care.

The oxygen content of the air in the loft decreases as a result of the birds' breathing, while its carbon dioxide content and humidity increases. **The air used up must be exchanged on a continuous basis**, and so great care must be taken that the loft has adequate ventilation. Even during the coldest of winters, continuous ventilation is vital, which must be achieved without any direct draught reaching the pigeons. **A pigeon can much more easily withstand cold but dry air than a warmer environment that is damp**.

All too often, fanciers have, in an attempt to protect their pigeons from cold winters, wrapped lofts up in plastic sheets almost to the point of making them airtight. This is not a good technique. In a loft wrapped up in plastic the air soon becomes saturated with humidity, which quickly turns to dew on the inside of the cold plastic. Water drips down everything, the feathers of the pigeons become moist and damp, a sure-fire path to illness. We should strive to prepare the buildings for winter with material that is permeable, but even in the case of buildings constructed from brick, we must regularly check to see that the ventilation is adequate. If we spot moisture within the loft, the level of ventilation must be increased.

Ammonia is a strongly-smelling gas, the presence of which suggests overcrowding or inadequate ventilation or cleaning. It is a poisonous gas which damages the nervous system and the surface of the mucosa, thus opening a point of weakness for pathogenic germs to attack. If we sense ammonia in the air, we should clean the loft more regularly, because the gas reaches the air from the droppings that accumulates on the floor. While it is no substitute for cleaning, afterwards it is very effective to scatter **zeolite** on the floor. This mineral substance adsorbs the harmful gases, not only outside the body, but also within it, and so it is also beneficial when applied internally.

It is also of beneficial effect if we scatter **clean, dry sand** over the floor of the loft, and clean it away regularly. When removing the used sand we also remove huge amounts of pathogens, bacteria, viruses and parasites. (The sand removed in this way is to be considered dirty, infectious material, and so provisions need to be taken for its appropriate disposal – e.g. burying it – or for it to be cleaned of its offensive content! Under no circumstance may the flock of chickens around the house be allowed to pick at the material brought out of the loft!)

Overcrowding and the subsequent degradation of air quality can cause the flaring up of respiratory diseases caused by **mycoplasmas**. This pathogen, as we will see in greater detail in the relevant section, is typically a secondary attacker of a system already weakened by other factors. Thus whenever mycoplasmal illness appears, we must always look for the primary cause that has given rise to it – usually we will find it in the form of some kind of **hygiene fault**.

Feeding

The qualitative and quantitative aspects of feeding are as much of primary importance in pigeon-breeding as elsewhere, but the details of this are outside the scope of this book. Here I merely raise the reader's attention to the fact that careful attention must be paid to the feed being **free from mould**! Many types of mould fungi produce toxins, that is poisons, which can directly damage crucial organs and cause serious harm to the reproductive organs. Visibly mouldy or fusty-smelling feed must not be given to birds! Another possible sign of mould fungi in otherwise seemingly good feed is **if a large part or all of the flock rejects it**. Feed that is infected with fungi or their toxins must not be given to any kind of animal, and needs – bearing in mind environmental regulations – to be destroyed.

Provision of water

Critical in pigeon-breeding as elsewhere is the guaranteed provision of ample, clean, fresh, pathogen-free drinking water. Regular replacement of water, and keeping drinkers clean, is also highly important, because infected water is one of the most common ways for pathogens to pass from one pigeon to another. If an infected pigeon drinks from the drinker, pathogens flow into the water from its beak and buccal cavity, which survive and spread, eventually infecting the entire flock.

We can prevent infection transferred through water in a number of ways. We should change the water as often as reasonably possible, if necessary putting more drinkers in the loft. **Acidification** of drinking water also helps, because it is precisely bacteria like salmonella, which cause the greatest problems for pigeon owners, that find it hardest to survive the acidic agents. **Apple vinegar** has long been used to acidify water, but there are also factory-made products which contain many different acids in optimal proportions. These not only prevent certain bacteria from spreading in the drinking water, but also keep them in check within the digestive system itself, and also have a beneficial effect on digestion of feed. Of natural vinegars, it is the apple vinegar that is best recommended; factory products generally contain a mixture of acetic acid, lactic acid and citric acid. The acidification of drinking water is an economical procedure, allowing us to **spare ourselves a lot of antibiotic treatment**, which is not only beneficial financially, but also environmentally and from the perspective of our own health, as we will see in greater detail later.

The usual dose of apple vinegar of natural origin and 5% concentration is 6-8ml per litre of drinking water, i.e. slightly less than a tablespoon per litre of water.

Note

In hot weather the pigeons' rate of breathing speeds up greatly: hyperventilation can result in too much carbon dioxide leaving the body, swinging the pH level of the blood in an alkaline direction. In the long term this can even be fatal, and so it is particularly beneficial if the inclusion of acidic material helps keep the pH of the blood in balance.

*

Some fanciers recommend disinfection of drinking water with bleach (sodium hypochloride), using a concentration of one tablespoon of hypo for each five litres of water. This can cause concern, however, for it is precisely the salmonellas that cause paratyphoid that are principally transmitted orally, and it is gently alkaline, watery environments that they like the best – in such circumstances they are even capable of growing. And bleach and similar compounds leave an alkaline pH level in their wake. It seems much more logical to treat drinking water with organic acids and vinegars, and practical experience bears this out.

Drinkers

We can use many kinds of drinker for providing water; whether home-made or purchased, what matters is that it be as easy as possible for the pigeons to reach the drinking water, and as hard as possible for them to make it dirty. Also important from the point of view of animal hygiene is the material the drinker is made of, for this dictates its **disinfectability**.

Drinkers used to be made out of clay, stone, wood, and then from metal; nowadays they are increasingly made of plastic. Drinkers made of clay are not easy to clean: bacteria can hide in the clay's tiny pores, making them hard to reach with disinfectant. Cracked wooden drinkers present similar worries. Drinkers made of stone or marble are not widespread, neither are they very practical, but there is no doubt that these are the natural materials that are the easiest to clean.

Metal drinkers can be easily and effectively disinfected, but they also have a disadvantage: certain types of liquids can dissolve metal ions from them, whose effect can be harmful. The **metal ions** entering the solution, for example, can sometimes interact with certain medicines and vaccinations, reducing their effectiveness. For this reason, especially in hot weather, water with medicine dissolved in it must not be left to stand in metal drinkers. We often give our pigeons vinegar, and so we should be aware that even weak acids like apple vinegar solution can chemically react with metals, which can cause an adverse level of metal intake through the drinking water. Particularly dangerous from this perspective are brass drinkers, for copper can have a very adverse effect on the liver. If metal trays are used, then, we recommend ones that are **zinc-plated**, or, ideally, **enamelled**.

Plastic drinkers are very practical. They are cheap and light, though their cleaning is more difficult than that of good quality zinc-plated metal ones, especially if they have been used to hold water containing medicines or vitamins. They are widely available, because there is a widespread notion that plastic is the substance that can most easily be disinfected, and that pathogens are incapable of settling on it.

It is not certain that this is the case, and recently doubt has been cast on a belief that has been held for decades. For it has been shown that in a comparison of plastic and wooden cutting boards used in kitchens, many fewer pathogens were able to reside in the wooden surface than on the plastic one, however much simpler it might seem to clean. Research into the precise reason for this continues, but it seems likely that even when treated, natural wood possesses a defence system that is effective against intruding microorganisms even in dead wood cells.

Cleaning and disinfecting

Within the loft, pathogens spread among the pigeons **in three main ways**: by air, by water, and through faeces.

It is virtually impossible to prevent airborne transfer. (This is why it is necessary immediately to remove specimens that are visibly ill, and releasing pathogens in great quantities.) We have already discussed waterborne transfer. It is transfer through faeces that has the greatest practical significance. Firstly, because the pathogens of almost all infectious diseases are released in faeces in large quantities, and secondly because pathogens are "safe" inside the excrement, where they can even remain with the potential to infect for a number of months.

Pigeons need a dry, clean environment, which can primarily be achieved with regular cleaning. The droppings accumulating on the floor need to be removed at least every other day, but in the event of illness in the loft this should be as often as several times a day. We should clean the quarantine on a daily basis, but – in line with the recommendations above – the tasks in the quarantine should always be left to the end of the day. (If possible, on any given day, we should not go back from the quarantine to the healthy birds.)

Regular disinfection is an absolute requirement, but we should be quick to add that it is no substitute for cleaning. The germs survive inside the faeces that have accumulated on the floor and the equipment, even if we use the strongest of disinfectants. The active ingredients are essentially only effective at surface level, and their penetrative capacity is only a few millimetres at most. Therefore disinfection must always be preceded by thorough cleaning, when we remove the dried, accumulated dirt (which is best done with thorough soaking); that is, **we disinfect a building and objects that are already clean**.

*

When the building "becomes tired"

Any breeder of animals will know that no amount of cleaning and disinfection will stop certain infectious diseases from becoming increasingly regular, and therefore with time the animal stock will perform less and less well. This is particularly evident in the case of large-scale animal stocks, but can also be observed on a smaller scale in pigeon lofts. It is on such occasions that we say that the building has become tired.

The main reason for this phenomenon is that despite effective cleaning and disinfection, **pathogens gradually accumulate** within the building. With time, small and large cracks develop on the walls, the floor, the equipment, and various pieces of furniture. More and more germs hide in these cracks and survive disinfection, and the pathogens remain in greater and greater numbers, cause disease increasingly often. This is compounded by the fact that the sensitivity of particular pathogens to particular disinfectants varies, and if we do not swap the disinfectants we use from time to time, certain types of pathogens are capable of becoming much more abundant.

With a little attention, it is easy to defend against this latter danger. Nowadays a large selection of disinfectants are available, and it is advisable to vary them on a systematic basis. It is harder to defend against the ageing of the building. Some breeders choose the option of burning, using an open flame (e.g. a gas-burner) to burn suitable – inflammable! – surfaces. It is a very dangerous technique, one that in many instances is entirely unsuitable.

A risk-free and effective method is the **annual replacement of the ground** under the loft and the aviary, naturally only where this is earth or sand (and where there are suitable solutions for the disposal of the infected soil!). In the case of concrete floors, we recommend they **be soaked over a number of days with strong disinfectant**. Finally, where practicable, a very effective technique is **to leave particular buildings and lofts unused for a certain period**. On such occasions, we move the birds to another loft, clean and disinfect thoroughly, then leave the building 'to rest' for months, maybe even one or two years – i.e. leave it completely empty, and not let any animal enter. During the rest period we repeat the disinfection process every month or two.

*

Please note!

I would again like to draw your attention to the fact that **whitewashing is not an adequate means of disinfection**! Firstly, lime has little effect on certain pathogens; secondly, after a time the whitewashed surface will be weakly but continuously alkaline, and **a weakly alkaline environment is particularly favourable for the survival of salmonellas and coli bacteria**!

These bacteria like precisely this gently alkaline environment, while in acidic conditions they decay quickly. For this reason – alongside the acidification of drinking water – systematic cleaning of the loft, or spraying the walls with slightly vinegarish water, can prove extremely effective.

*

The various types of disinfectants are generally **poisonous** to some degree for warm-blooded animals, and hence also for pigeons. This is also the case for humans, of course. To avoid the risk of accidents, we should always read the product instructions with the greatest care! We should take great care with poisonous gases or vapours that may accumulate as a result of the use of certain substances, particularly in closed spaces! This can even occur when using a strongly vinegarish solution!

3. The immune system and stress

The body is under continuous attack from the outside world, in the form of various pathogens (viruses, bacteria, fungi, parasites), which it must defend against on a continuous basis. Internal defence is also required, for example against continuously developing tumour cells. The body is defended against internal and external attacks by its **immune system**. Inadequate operation of the **defence system** can quickly cause disease or even death.

By immunity we mean the body's defence against pathogens or diseases. We can talk in terms of specific immunity, when we examine the body's status with regard to one particular pathogen, for example if we see whether a certain pigeon is protected against paramyxovirus. But we can also speak of the general level of the body's immune state, by which we mean the level of immune response of a given specimen at a given moment, that is, the defence reaction it can produce to the various pathogens attacking it.

The **immune response** is an extremely complicated process, a detailed description of which is certainly outside the scope of this book. In very general terms, we can say that **the body responds to the attacks in two stages:**

1. **identification of the pathogen**
2. **defence against it**

The immune system is capable of recognizing the body's own cells and alien cells that are unlike them. If it identifies an alien cell, it begins a complicated process during which it strives to destroy and remove the pathogens. The entirety of these processes, that is **the speed and success of the immune response, depends on the state of the immune system, and on whether or not the body has previously encountered the same (or a similar!) pathogen**.

The speed of immune processes

If a pathogen (e.g. a virus or bacterium) attacks the body, a race effectively begins against time. Having attacked the body, the bacteria and viruses begin fast reproduction, destroying more and more cells and pieces of tissue. If the body is not capable of defending against them **fast enough**, it cannot keep pace with the pathogens, and this handicap can cause the body to become seriously ill or even die.

If the body is attacked by a pathogen that **it has never encountered before**, it takes a relatively **long time** to identify it, "take a sample of it", and begin producing appropriate antibodies. This can take days, during which the spreading pathogens can gain advantage, even outright superiority. If a pigeon is infected with paramyxovirus, for example, and has never encountered the pathogen before (neither has it been previously infected, nor vaccinated), the virus can begin almost limitless multiplication on the first infection, because the pigeon's body not only lacks the specific **antiviral substance**, but does not even have the necessary **information** about the virus at its disposal. The result of such an infection is serious disease and often death.

Assuming a healthy immune system, we can say that **the immune response to an infection is faster and stronger if the body has encountered the pathogen previously**. On such occasions, the identification of the pathogen and in particular the production of antibodies takes place much more quickly, and the body defeats the infection at its embryonic stage, before the pathogens are given much of a chance to propagate. We could equally say that the immune system is "introduced" to this particular pathogen.

This "introduction" can take place in the course of **natural infection**, when the body becomes ill, but succeeds in defeating the illness. This we describe as **natural immunity**. When it next meets the pathogen, the body is capable of reacting quickly, and in most instances this prevents even minor symptoms of the illness from appearing.

This natural immunity is a so-called **acquired immunity**. Also acquired is **artificially induced immunity**. This can be achieved by means of various **inoculations and vaccinations**. This means that killed or weakened pathogens (or certain parts of them) are artificially introduced into the exposed body, for example by injection under the skin (in the case of paramyxovirus) or by being rubbed into feather follicles (in the case of pigeon pox). **The killed or weakened virus or bacterium** is not capable of propagation in any great quantity, or of causing illness in the body, but **does carry valuable information about itself**. This information is processed and stored by the body, then used in the event of a real infection: with its help, it will defend itself more quickly and more effectively than a body than has not been vaccinated. It is this **increased speed** and effectiveness which **decides** whether the body defeats the illness or only develops it slightly, or whether it fails to survive it.

The duration of the acquired immunity

There is great variation in the time for which the immunity acquired from different pathogens is sustained, and this primarily **depends on the type of the pathogen**. No lasting defence can develop against the mycoplasmas, for example, while immunity induced by pox virus (whether natural or vaccine) usually lasts a lifetime.

While there are exceptions, in general natural immunity is longer-lasting than that induced artificially by vaccination. There are a number of reasons for this, one of the prime ones being that vaccination introduces dead or weakened pathogens into the body, which generate an immune response and therefore protection, but this will not usually be of the same degree as the immunity acquired from the survival of an illness caused by a "wild" pathogen. This is one reason why, for example, **we must vaccinate against paramyxovirus on an annual basis**, for even the strongest vaccines are not capable of providing protection for a longer period.

It is important to note that artificially induced immunity needs time to develop. This time is typically 10-14 days. In other words, **we can only expect protection about two weeks after a vaccination is given**.

We should also be aware that the protection provided by vaccination can be increased by a so-called booster shot or reminder shot: we can achieve greater and longer-lasting protection against the given pathogen if we repeat the vaccination after a certain period (a few weeks).

The recommended times for vaccinations and booster shots will be discussed individually along with the diseases in question.

*

The degree of artificial protection and the success (or lack of success) of vaccinations

In general, pigeons that have been vaccinated, that is immunized, acquire protection against the disease targeted by the vaccination in question. It is highly important for us to know, however, that **this artificially induced protection is never 100% guaranteed**! Not for one individual specimen, and **certainly not for the flock as a whole**.

Below we list the factors that can cause pigeons to develop a disease despite having been vaccinated against it. For greater clarity, we will take injections against the disease caused by the paramyxovirus as an example. (*We will return to the following factors in greater detail later in the book.*)

Reasons for vaccinated pigeons later developing the disease:

<u>Errors in vaccination</u>

- inadequate vaccine: use of vaccines containing the wrong strain of paramyxovirus (made for other animal species)

- vaccine past its expiry date

- vaccine that is in principle still valid, but that has been stored incorrectly

- injection in the wrong place (e.g. within skin, in the air)

- injection at the wrong time (when specimen is ill or exhausted)

- polluted syringe (active ingredient is ruined)

- specimen infected with parasites

- wrong vaccination dose (inadequate amount of vaccine administered)

- vaccine ruined (put in water that is too hot before being injected)

- specimen accidentally left out (specimens mixed up at time of vaccination)

- specimen left out for other reasons (e.g. pigeon not in yard at time of vaccination)

<u>Errors unrelated to vaccination</u>

Pathogen-related:

- overwhelming infection, attack of too great a mass of pathogens at once, which is capable of breaking through even the protection provided by the vaccination

- long-lasting, continuous infection, which exhausts the immune system

- attack of a particularly wild strain of the virus or bacterium, which is more virulent than the average

- a mutation, or transformation, of the virus

- attack of a bacterium of the same type as the vaccine but of a different subtype (e.g. a new strain of salmonella imported from abroad)

Because of inadequate operation of the immune system:

- metabolic causes (e.g. lack of selenium)

- presence of circovirus infection

- individual, congenital immune deficiency

From the above it is clear that innumerable errors can occur even during the vaccination. But even if there is no such negligence, **it is almost impossible that every member of our**

flock acquire protection from the vaccination. Again, this raises our attention to the fact that while localized protection or vaccination is essential, on its own – without **continuous prevention of epidemics and the necessary hygiene** – it is not enough to protect the health of the whole of the flock.

In addition to all of this, it is worth emphasizing that **vaccination will only be really effective if the immune system is operating at the highest possible level at the moment of injection and directly afterwards**. Nowadays various products are available (e.g. certain herbal extracts) which stimulate the body's immune response if administered at the same time as the vaccine, and this significantly raises the level of protection that the vaccination provides.

Emphasis is put on the above considerations because we often hear opinions to the effect that this or that vaccine is worthless, because even after vaccination some pigeons still developed the disease in question.

We have already presented the many possible reasons for this. We have seen how many things can go wrong with one vaccination, and in practice we cannot always avoid all of them. But even if we succeed in avoiding all the possible traps, **the effect of the vaccinations on the flock as a whole can never be 100% successful, due to individual differences in state of health, age, type, etc**. What is certain, however, is that a flock that has not been vaccinated will suffer far greater illness if infected than one that has been, even if we cannot guarantee complete protection for each individual specimen. And it is not insignificant whether 0% or say 95% of our flock is protected against a given disease.

*

We should mention that in addition to acquired immunity, there is another type of so-called species-specific immunity. For example: some pathogens do not make pigeons ill, not even if they are present in large numbers. Examples might be swine-fever or foot and mouth disease. These viruses are incapable of attaching themselves to the cells in a pigeon's body, incapable of propagation inside them, and thus not even theoretically capable of causing disease. (But it is important to note that for all this, pigeons can, in principle, carry and spread any kind of pathogen, by mechanical means if not by any other, e.g. in the form of dirt stuck on their feathers, which is a very significant issue from an epidemiological and human health perspective!)

There also exists age-related immunity. In the course of its development and growth, a specimen undergoes a number of changes, as a result of which its receptiveness to particular pathogens changes. For example the **circovirus** that attacks the immune system causes much less damage in adult pigeons than in younger ones, as with age certain immune organs (e.g. the Bursa of Fabricius) naturally become atrophied, and so the virus is incapable of multiplying within them.

Age-related immunity of the opposite kind can also be observed: in its first weeks of life, the young pigeon continues to be protected by the **maternal antibodies** passed on through the egg by the hen, and so the young temporarily enjoy (a certain) protection.

*

Deficient operation of the immune system

We can divide deficient operation of the immune system into two parts: relative deficiency and absolute deficiency.

Relative immune deficiency

If a body is in good health and **its immune system works well**, this generally provides enough defence against attack by pathogens; the body does not become ill, and it defeats attackers. If, under such circumstances, a disease nevertheless appears, there are two main possible explanations:

- **pathogens in too great numbers; massive infection**
- **attack by pathogens that are as yet unknown to the body**

We discussed the second possibility at the start of the section. And during our discussion of hygiene we saw that even if the immune system works well, after a heavy, massive infection, when pathogens enter the body in huge numbers, the immune system quickly becomes exhausted, and is no longer capable of defending the body. Thus it is crucial that, by continuously maintaining hygiene and taking steps to prevent infection, we keep the number of pathogens in the pigeons' environment to a minimum.

Absolute immune deficiency

We refer to absolute immune inadequacy when for some reason the body's defence system **does not operate properly**. This means that when a pathogen enters the body, whether it is known or not, the immune system does not operate as it should, resulting in the body becoming ill, or dying.

There can be many reasons why the immune system does not operate adequately. We do not deal with inherited disorders in the book, while the causes of specific diseases (e.g. circovirus, metabolic illnesses) are discussed in the respective sections. Here we turn to the immune system's enemy number one, the threat posed by **stress**.

Stress

The casual phrasing of the last sentence is quite deliberate: we would like to emphasize that stress is a collective term, by which and in association with which we can list a large number of things. If we do however try to provide a brief definition of what we mean by stress, we would state that **stress is the aggregation of the effects produced by intrusions on the body**.

We are not left much the wiser by this, but we have learned that if this is the case, then the causes of stress also include **useful intrusions** to the body! For let us just think of sunshine, air, drinking water, feed: without all of these, living beings would not exist. But we must be aware that these factors **also carry with them the potential for adverse effects**. Overly strong sunshine causes cancer, as well as leading to hormonal problems; fresh air can be harmful, if it moves too quickly or happens to be too humid; drinking water that is too cold can indirectly cause illness; ingredients in feed represent a burden and potential danger, and certainly effort for the body before it has digested and excreted them.

So, among the causes of stress, we can list all the stimuli the outside world presents – so we have to find some kind of basis of comparison to decide whether they are useful or damaging for the body.

That is to say, we need stress, and without it we would not have life; everything around us acts as a stressor, a cause of stress. Whether a stressor is adverse or beneficial is decided by the body's reaction, which in turn is determined by the **stressor's magnitude**. It is highly likely that this is the point of reference which can help us find our way in the labyrinth of stress.

Let us take a look at an example! Let us imagine someone sitting in a comfortable armchair positioned in the middle of an empty room, and observe their behaviour as we play them some pleasant music. Provided the music does not exceed a certain volume, it has a pleasant, that is good, effect on the listener. But if we turn up the volume from the speakers, the music will eventually lose its pleasant effect, and become increasingly uncomfortable: **there will be too much of it**. If on the other hand we turn the volume down too low, it will be impossible to enjoy it, as **it will not reach the necessary stimulus quantity** needed to elicit a pleasant response. If we turn the music off completely, it elicits no response at all, and sooner or later it will be precisely the stimulus-free environment that will stimulate our imagined experimental subject.

We can conduct this experiment with everything that surrounds us: noise, light, food and drink, medicine, sport, even a relationship with a person of the opposite sex. The result we get is the same: **stimuli from the outside world are essential for an individual to survive, but in excessive quantities they are just as damaging as if insufficient or absent**.

To return to the topic of this book, we can take an example from the field of diseases: the continual presence of a small amount of pathogens is useful for the immune system, because it keeps it in a constant state of awareness, of "being prodded". When attacked by large numbers of pathogens, however, the immune system is exhausted, while the defence apparatus of a pigeon kept in sterile conditions for a prolonged period will become lazy to a dangerous degree. Similarly, an **underdose** of a vitamin or mineral substance is equally capable of causing illness or death as is an **overdose** of it. To take a ready example: if someone is kept on a stringent diet free of common salt, after a certain period their body risks disease or even death if it is not provided with enough chlorine and sodium – but if fed 200 grams of common salt, they would die within hours.

The immune system and stress

From the above it is no surprise that the continuous, satisfactory operation of the immune system demands constant stress effects, by which we mean stress effects that are useful and of suitable measure. In its everyday use, however, **the term 'stress' has an entirely negative connotation**. If we are to say that our pigeons are stressed, we tend to mean that they are exposed to some kind of adverse influence (e.g. lengthy transportation), to which they respond negatively, and that we expect their general state to become less healthy as a result. While stress means much more than this, **within the confines of this book** we will keep to the everyday use of the term, defining stress as **a state that tends towards a more ill condition as a result of causes and circumstances that diverge from those that are familiar (ideal)**.

Let us see what happens to a pigeon in a state of stress! Stress leads to hormonal changes in its body that, beyond a certain point (whether in terms of time or magnitude), are damaging to certain organs, including the immune system. Stress suppresses and disables the immune system, one of the direct consequences of which is the temporary or ultimate victory of the pathogens over the body's defence mechanism. Under the effect of stress, the body can fall ill more quickly and more seriously if it happens to encounter external pathogens responsible for diseases.

Sadly, if the body is in a stressful state, some illnesses can develop without any new infection taking place. There are bacteria, fungi, parasites and viruses that are always present in healthy flocks and healthy specimens, which do not cause illness under normal circumstances because an **equilibrium** is established between them and their host's system. These **"cohabiters"** in the body can be found almost everywhere, equally in the intestines as on the mucous membrane of the upper respiratory tract, or inside or on the surface of the skin. If functioning well, the immune system keeps them in check, and so they are not capable of propagation in great quantities. If, however, **the defence provided by the immune system is weakened**, whether in general or locally (for example in the throat area after drinking cold water), **these germs are freed from these constraints and begin to multiply**, which will result in illness (in the above example, laryngitis).

The majority of the pathogens that induce illness in pigeons belong to this group, that of so-called **opportunistic pathogens**. To mention just a few examples, this group includes coccidia, mycoplasmas, trichomonads, various cocci, and herpesvirus; we could even add some strains of coli bacteria or the dreaded salmonella.

Maintaining the operation of the immune system

In pigeon-breeding, and particularly in pigeon-racing, there are countless factors that act as stressors on the birds. To mention but the most significant ones: pairing, raising the young, moulting, being encaged, transportation, races, vaccinations, extremes of climate, possible errors in housing (first and foremost, overcrowding), and of course regular attacks by a variety of pathogens. In particular, the immune systems of pigeons that are kept and raced **intensively** cannot take the heightened strain, the multitudes of stressors, and inevitably begin to weaken and become damaged. It is up to the pigeon fancier – especially if he expects a top performance from his flock – to maintain their immune systems at the necessary level.

This can be achieved in two main ways. If possible, **the number and size of harmful stressors must be decreased** through ideal housing and feeding. In addition, as there is a limit to the amount the stressors can be eliminated, **the pigeons' systems must be supported artificially**, particularly their immune systems. We describe the specific methods and preparations for this in the third and fourth chapters.

Note

Like humans, pigeons are not all alike. They react in different ways to the same stressor, and their response thresholds vary. For this reason, there will always be discrepancies in response within the flock: even if we keep and treat every member equally, there will be specimens that fall ill more quickly e.g. from mycoplasmosis, and there will be some that always outperform the others in races. Paying attention to variations from the average, both positive and negative – in terms of both health and performance – is one of the cornerstones of successful breeding.

*

Even with the strictest prevention of epidemics, the best hygiene, and an immune state maintained at a high level, what with intensive use, regular transportation, mixing, exhibiting and demanding races, the pigeons are **always balancing on the tightrope between health and illness as a result of their heavy use**. If we add the newly "imported" pathogens, primarily circovirus, which destroys the immune system, it can be no surprise that **nowadays there is an increasing need for preventive or healing treatment and medication of pigeons**.

It is far from trivial how this necessary preventive and healing treatment is carried out, however. **Often the therapy is destined to failure even before the medicine's packaging is even opened, and this failure can have a multitude of explanations!**

And it was with the intention of avoiding these failures that the second chapter was written.

II. General information about medicines

The continuous biomedical research of pharmaceutical companies has generated an unprecedented abundance and variety of veterinary products. There are currently many thousand veterinary medicines registered worldwide that can be officially distributed, not to mention the huge number of curative products on the market which do not count as medicines. Even if we only take a smaller region into account, there are many hundred products for use by the fanciers of a given country.

Clearly, finding one's bearings amongst so many products is no easy task, and one that without some basic knowledge is a hopeless one. The second part of the book discusses medicines and their use in a general sense; put another way, it introduces the reader to **a certain, easily-understood level of general pharmacology**. This knowledge will make it **easier to avoid the typical mistakes** that pigeon fanciers regularly make, however good their intentions. We will also eradicate the improper methods which unfortunately cause the "cultivation" of the strains of bacteria that resist medicines and scoff at antibiotics.

1. Medicines prior to use

Acquisition of medicines

We can group and classify veterinary medicines according to a number of criteria. According to one very practical such classification, there are preparations acquired without a prescription from a veterinarian (OTC products), and there are those which require a prescription or can only be acquired directly from the veterinarian. As their name suggests, these **prescription medicines** require the participation of a veterinarian both for purchase and use.

The proportion of products requiring a prescription varies from country to country. In most countries, antibiotics and other "strong" medicines require a prescription, but there are places where almost all products are freely acquired. That is to say, most fanciers have the option to treat their flocks or administer preventive medicine without recourse to a veterinarian. In the interests of the fancier's wallet and of protecting pigeons' health, however, I should mention some risks presented by inadequate healing attempts conducted in the absence of a professional. (I should be quick to add that even apparently simple, routine preventive treatment can be appallingly mishandled.)

First of all, **the pre-requisite of efficient and economical treatment is a precise, applicable diagnosis!** That is, the determination of the problem the specimen or the flock has, that which we have to protect against. It is unwise to begin "treatment" without a well-established diagnosis, as it means trusting things to luck. And luck, as we know, has its downs as well as its ups.

Establishing the right diagnosis is often no easy task, and in most instances requires special tests in addition to a thorough physical exam. Such **tests** include:

- diagnostic dissection

- parasitological tests
- bacterial cultures
- susceptibility tests
- blood tests
- histological tests
- other, specialized tests

This list begins with everyday (routine) tests that are easy to carry out, and that can be performed in most veterinary surgeries. At the end are the more expensive techniques that demand serious laboratory equipment, which are used less frequently, but which in many cases are nevertheless essential.

Dissection, parasitological tests, bacterial cultures and susceptibility tests are all fast and relatively cheap procedures. In the vast majority of cases they are adequate for a precise diagnosis to be established, but they also **assist in choosing the most effective medicine**. These tests cost money, of course, but this is often less than the cost of a single dose of medicine we might acquire "blind", the use of which may not only be ineffective but may also further worsen the health of our flock. And such a situation can only be rectified, or improved, (if at all) at the cost of repeated financial losses including removal of the sick birds.

(In addition to this, growing bacterial cultures and parasitological tests in particular provide highly useful information about the **current immune state** of the specimen or the flock.)

Fanciers often approach me with the usual "medical history": "We have tried every type of medicine, nothing worked, now what should we give them?" When they list all the things they have bombarded their pigeons with, and their doses – **in the absence of a diagnosis** – it is a wonder the birds have survived at all. Dissecting one such deceased pigeon, we can see the damage inflicted on the internal organs of the unfortunate bird by medicines administered in good faith but in a haphazard fashion. It had long not been the original disease the pigeon had suffered from, but the adverse side-effects of **medicines given in poisonous doses and combinations**.

So medical treatment generally begins with a veterinary exam, then continues with the diagnosis, after which the veterinarian will usually write a prescription or two, hand them to the owner, and send him to the animal pharmacy. The fancier can then visit the first such pharmacy and purchase the product, but equally he can exercise his democratic right to throw away the prescription and try to acquire the medicine by other means. Indeed, he can even leave out the veterinarian as a necessary evil, and follow his own advice or that of his colleagues, which on many occasions will no doubt have good results.

It is worth bearing some considerations in mind, however. Firstly, wherever we find the medicine, we should only purchase it if it is offered in its **original manufacturer's packaging**. I have seen countless re-packaged drugs for sale at fairs, markets and exhibitions, with at best the name of the medicine in the packet, or what its seller claims is in it. Maybe it was very good medicine, but we may equally have acquired medicine for our flock that is:

- past its expiry date
- still valid, but no longer effective (wrong storage)
- diluted
- counterfeit
- lucky not to be poisonous
- from a questionable source
- with some other fault

The possibilities are almost endless.

We should have the same reservations regarding medicines given to us with the best intentions by friends and fellow association members, but whose qualities, and therefore effect on the flock, are unknown. I have experienced many situations in which the breeder has treated his birds with drugs he knows nothing about. Another common occurrence is that fanciers insist on finding the same medicine that they happened to use last year: it is by no means sure that it will have as good an effect this year, as the state of health of the flock may have changed enormously in the meanwhile.

It is a general recommendation that medicine only be bought in its original packaging, and from a place where its **suitable storage** is guaranteed. Such places include animal pharmacies and surgeries of veterinarians with licences to dispense medicines.

The method of **transportation** is also very important, i.e. the journey the medicine makes from the producer to the pharmacy, and from the pharmacy to the user. Sending medicines by post, for example, is not recommended, if the temperature range within which the drug retains its effectiveness cannot be guaranteed for the whole route. In other words, the medicine can be ruined in transit if it is exposed to extremes of heat or cold.

We should also be take precautions when taking home medicines purchased in the pharmacy. In the winter, products transported in the boot of the car can **freeze**, while if put inside the car, even winter sunshine can **overheat** them through the glass. The risk of the latter is even greater in summer, of course. Because of this, for longer trips it is advisable to put heat-sensitive vaccines and probiotics in coolers (but not in a freezer); but even for shorter journeys we should at least put them in a number of layers of plastic bag and tie them up, which provides temporary protection from changes in temperature.

If warmed above twenty degrees centigrade (68°F), **vaccines can lose their effectiveness** in a matter of hours, and above fifty degrees (122°F) **in a matter of minutes**: although they display no alteration to the naked eye, their immunizing power is nullified – and, sadly, this will only transpire when the illness appears. (This can be one of the reasons the fancier watches his flock, dumbfounded as to why, after orderly and timely vaccination, it has nevertheless become infected.) Neither do vitamins appreciate high temperatures: above fifty degrees (122°F) they begin quickly to deteriorate, and they can easily warm up to this extent on the backseat of a car parked in the blazing sun. This is equally true of antibiotics; indeed, some must be stored below room temperature, i.e. transported in cooler bags and kept in the refrigerator at home.

Home storage of medicines

Pharmaceutical companies always describe, in its official specification and on the packaging, how a medicine should be stored, and it is advisable to observe this. **Improper storage can quickly and easily ruin the medicine**, which at best can cause its effectiveness to decline or disappear, and at worst can mean that harmful materials form in a product otherwise designed to heal.

Vaccines aside, the description of most products states “Store in a dry, cool place” or “Store in a dry place at room temperature”. Many also add “Store away from bright light”. It is worth complying with these relatively undemanding requirements, else our weapon in the fight against disease loses its edge even before it is introduced.

It is clear from these storage recommendations that there are three factors which most affect the period for which medicines retain their effectiveness:

a) temperature
b) humidity
c) (light) radiation

a) Temperature

As a good rule of thumb, with every temperature increase of 10 degrees Celsius (18°F) the period of a particular chemical and physical process is halved, i.e. the process becomes twice as fast. (This is also true in reverse, of course: a reduction in temperature slows the process in the same measure.) For example, everyone will have seen at first hand how medicines dissolve more easily in warm than in cold water. But they also disintegrate more quickly in the warm than in colder conditions, and so it is important that we observe the prescribed temperature range.

For the majority of medicines, and particularly vaccines, overly cold temperatures (freezing) are also highly detrimental. (Most vaccines should be kept at a temperature of 2-8°C (36-46°F).) We should always follow the instructions on the packaging.

Freezing ruins most medicines dissolved in a **liquid**. This is often visible to the naked eye, as after thawing the liquid becomes cloudy and breaks up, i.e. the individual ingredients precipitate in it. But even if a medicine suffers no observable damage in the cold, it may lose its effectiveness, and so we should not leave it in an unheated room in winter for any period of time.

b.) Humidity

In this instance, humidity means the **dampness of the air** surrounding the medicine. In general, the original packaging is not permeable, but of course it becomes so once opened, and in overly damp conditions the medicine "soaks it up", usually causing its disintegration and loss of effectiveness. Some products are so sensitive to damp that they are capable of extracting water from the air even under normal dry conditions. A good example of this is clavulanic acid. The manufacturer includes absorbent material in the medicine's packaging, to protect it from the humidity in the air. After administering the daily dose, we should take care to seal the remaining medicine properly, in an airtight fashion, with the absorbent sachet alongside it, else it will lose its effectiveness by the following day.

If we use powdered medicine supplied in a packet, we can best protect the remaining material after measuring out the daily dose by folding back the opening, fastening it with a rubber band, putting it in a sealable jar, then placing it in a cool, dry place. The refrigerator does not count as a dry place, and so we should only keep opened medicines there if in airtight containers.

On the subject of refrigerators, attention should be drawn to the fact that medicines should only be stored such that **it should not be easy for unauthorized persons to get at them (even by accident)**. Here I am thinking of an unsuspecting member of the family mistaking a medicine stored in the fridge or the larder, perhaps no longer in its original packaging, for food, e.g. for flour, and using it accordingly. Therefore we should store medicines such that there is no chance of others, **PARTICULARLY CHILDREN**, getting at them. The ideal is to designate a separate cupboard for medicines, that we fix high up on the wall in a cool, dry room, and protect with a lock. In the absence of a separate refrigerator we must use the family one for the storage of medicines sensitive to heat, and in this case it is advisable to put them in a sealed little box that children are not able to open.

c.) Light radiation

The majority of active ingredients disintegrate when they come into contact with certain types of radiation. As light is a form of – electromagnetic – radiation, most medicines cannot withstand it, particularly **direct sunlight**. As strong artificial light can also be detrimental, it is best to store medicines in systematized boxes that are well-sealed and whose sides do not let light in.

The expiry date of medicines

The expiry date is marked on the packaging of veterinary products: this is the date until which the medicine will "certainly" maintain its quality. We put the word "certainly" in inverted commas because this is only true if the product is stored in the proper fashion.

Naturally, every effort should be made to purchase and use up the medicine before its expiry date, but we should be aware that this is all relative. It may be that one medicine, though theoretically a few days or weeks past its expiry date, will be more effective than one that has not expired but has been stored incorrectly. For example, in many places it is customary for the manufacturer to collect unsold medicines and vaccines that are past their expiry date, make an official test of their effectiveness, and if they prove to be faultless, extend the date stated. (This is of course marked on the packaging of the product.)

In the same way, if vitamins stored at home are a week or two, perhaps a month past their expiry date, but we are certain that they have been stored properly, we should feel free to use them, as they will still be effective. And this is true in reverse, too: if we have a medicine that has theoretically not yet expired, but we know that it was stored wrongly (e.g. in a very warm room in summer, or in a refrigerator, but not sealed), it is better to dispose of it, as it is almost certain to be ineffective, and may even cause illness.

Often we do not use products in powder form in one go, but only take out smaller amounts at a time. It is vital that the tool we use to reach into the packet be **clean and dry**, otherwise, e.g. with a wet spoon, we can ruin what is left in it. At worst, with a dirty utensil, we could even infect the medicine.

The jars of products in liquid form should be carefully resealed after use, otherwise part of the solvent in which they are dissolved may evaporate. This causes the medicine in the jar to thicken, meaning that there is much more of the active ingredient per unit of volume, with which we can even poison our flock. On no account should liquids be frozen, as this causes their ingredients to separate and be ruined. A similar phenomenon can be observed without freezing: individual components can separate from the overcooled and thereby oversaturated solution, and become crystallized. If we then carefully warm up the medicine (e.g. by taking it indoors), the separated ingredient may dissolve again – in which case the product can still be used. Failing this, unfortunately, we have to dispose of it.

Note

Ruined medicine that is past its expiry date, leftovers and even empty packaging should be treated as hazardous waste! They should be transported to suitable places to be processed, and until then they must be sealed such that there is no chance of an unauthorized person, particularly a child, having access to them!

*

Keeping a flock diary is very useful, if not indispensable, not just to keep a record of medicines and treatments, but also for other reasons. Any large notebook is suitable for this purpose, in which we can write down all the activities and events relating to our pigeon flock. The diary can include preventive treatments, vitamins administered, times of vaccinations, illnesses occurring, veterinary tests, acquisition of medicines, doses of medicines used and the time they are administered, adding the observed effectiveness of the treatment, acts of disinfection, buying and selling of pigeons, as well as exhibitions, races, results achieved, etc. Keeping a diary of this kind proves useful even in the short term, but it can also be highly instructive to flick through it years later.

2. Administering medicines

Once the precise diagnosis has been established, and the most effective medicine acquired, the treatment of the specimen or flock can begin – with the participation of the veterinarian or on the basis of his recommendations. As the veterinarian cannot be present in person each time a medicine is administered, and as, with time, his instructions begin to be forgotten, it is vital that the fancier have a knowledge of the basics of health care.

We discuss the use of medicines according to three main considerations:

- **mode by which medicines are administered**
- **dosage**
- **time and duration of the medicine's application**

Mode by which medicines are administered

In practical terms, medicines can be divided up into those for **internal** and those for **external** use. We must note, however, that some products for external use, by seeping through the skin, also have an effect internally, while the task of a significant number of internal medicines is to protect the bird's covering, its skin and plumage. **The place a medicine is administered is not always the same as where it has its effect**.

1. Products for **external** use:
- powders
- sprays
- bathing agents
- fluids to be dripped onto the skin
- eye drops, eye creams

2. Products for **internal** use:
- those administered orally
- those that are injected
- those that are inhaled (taken in through breathing)

1. Products for external use

Powders

Powders are used against external parasites. The product is applied directly to the body of the pigeon or to parts of the loft (e.g. nests), as removed from the packet, without dilution.

Advantages

Does not require preparation, there are no leftovers to dispose of, pigeons can be treated one at a time.

Disadvantages

Rising into the air, the powder contaminates the surroundings, and breathing it in can be dangerous for the user. If the powder is put in a damp place, it becomes clotted up and loses its effectiveness. The pigeons must be treated individually, which makes it very time-consuming if there are many birds, and disturbs the flock. It does not protect the whole of the body's surface.

Sprays

For use against external parasites. They can also be found in smaller handheld flasks, where the active ingredient can be pumped at the pigeon directly. Traditional sprays must be diluted before being transferred to a flask or backpack sprayer and applied to the pigeons or the loft.

Advantages

Sprays generally attach themselves to the plumage better than powder does, and their effect is more prolonged. Damp conditions do not pose much of a problem. Releasing the spray is much less time-consuming. In the form of a handheld flask it is ideal for smaller-scale treatment (e.g. in a quarantine).

Disadvantages

The mist or vapour of the spray is harmful for both pigeon and breeder if it is breathed in or reaches the eyes. It can pollute the environment of the loft. When treating the entire flock, a handheld spray is time-consuming, while the liquid emitted by a backpack sprayer does not reach the depths of the plumage.

Bathing agents

Whether it is in solid or liquid form, we dilute the product in water in a given proportion, then dip the pigeons in the solution or leave them to bathe in it.

Advantages

Of those mentioned so far, this is the method that has the greatest effect. The active ingredient reaches the entire surface of the pigeon (except its head), and remains there for a prolonged period.

Disadvantages

Can only be used in warm periods. The leftover soaking solution is dangerous residue, and special care must be taken with its disposal.

Warning!

When acquiring and using bathing products and sprays, we should make sure they are harmless to pigeons! It is not unknown for pigeons to have been treated and killed with products harmless to some mammals but highly poisonous to birds!

Fluids to be dripped onto the skin

Most recently, antiparasitic products have appeared on the market which have not previously been suitable for pigeons, but have successfully been used for years on dogs and cats. Depending on the bird's size, one or more drops should be dripped onto the surface of the pigeon's skin. The active ingredient spreads across the entire surface of the skin, and, seeping through the skin into the body, effectively destroys internal and external parasites alike.

Advantages

Causes the least damage to the environment and does not harm the fancier's health. Can be measured out precisely and reliably, and is ideal for individual application (quarantine). Not weather-dependent, it can also be used in the cold. It does not get into the eyes or irritate the conjunctiva. Also effective against parasites living in the surroundings that only occasionally attack the pigeons.

Disadvantages

The members of the flock must be treated one by one.

Warning!

With all of the techniques listed above, we must also protect our own health! We should always use rubber gloves, and also wear a breathing mask and safety glasses when using sprays and powders!

Eye drops, eye creams

These are products, usually containing antibiotics, which we drip or spread directly onto the conjunctival sac once or twice a day, continuously for a number of successive days. We must pay heightened attention to cleanliness when using them, and avoid the product becoming contaminated! Between applications, the product should be kept in a refrigerator, but even there it will expire within a few weeks.

Only products specifically suitable for the eyes, no other drips or creams, should be used!

2. Products for internal use

Medicines administered orally

The most common form of administering medicine is by mouth. This can be done:

- mixed into drinking water
- mixed into food
- individually

The advantage of the first two methods is that they involve minimal work and disturbance of the flock, while their disadvantage is that they are inaccurate – it is not sure that each specimen will receive an adequate amount of the active ingredient. The third technique avoids this problem, but if it has to be used over a long period, particularly if more than once a day, it is time-consuming and very tiring – for both the flock and the owner.

Many active ingredients administered by mouth **are not absorbed from the gut**, and thus only have an effect inside the intestinal system. (This is true of certain antibiotics, e.g. gentamycin, streptomycin, neomycin, colistin, and spectinomycin.) These can have a beneficial effect in the event of intestinal inflammation, but if the pathogens are (already) outside the intestinal canal and attacking other organs, medicines not absorbed from the gut cannot reach them. If we want their effect to reach the whole of the body, we must apply them in a different fashion (e.g. by injection).

Medicines mixed in drinking water

This is the most practical mode of administering medicine. It makes treatment of the whole flock quick and easy. Compared to mixing with food, it has the advantage that while **ill birds** eat little or no food, in most cases they still **drink water**, and are thus more likely to receive the medicine.

Its disadvantage is that some medicines have an unpleasant taste when dissolved in water, and so the pigeons are only willing to drink them after **being made thirsty beforehand**, which strongly affects them as a stressor. Naturally, a further disadvantage is that some active ingredients are not soluble (e.g. metronidazole). Also, consumption of water is subject to significant **fluctuation** depending on temperature and other circumstances, and the amount of medicine taken in fluctuates likewise. Furthermore, some medicines perish quickly in lukewarm solution, so we should only prepare a small amount of fresh solution at a time, repeating this more often in hot weather.

Medicines mixed into food

This is generally used for preventive treatment, when the (majority of the) flock is not yet ill. Its advantage is that a large amount can be mixed in at once, requiring little in the way of extra labour.

In the case of pigeon-breeding, however, it has the obvious disadvantage that pigeons tend to consume seed, with which it is difficult to mix a product that is in powder form. One solution is if the drug is mixed into granulated feed in the course of production (medicated, vitamin-enriched feed), but this practice, unlike with other animal species, is not yet widespread in the case of pigeons.

Unless applied on an individual basis, however, we have no choice but to mix insoluble products into the birds' feed. With powdered medicines, this takes place as follows: we slightly moisten the daily portion of feed for the birds we wish to treat (sprinkling a tablespoon or two of water on a kilogram of feed), stir it, then scatter the daily dose of medicine on it, and, carefully but thoroughly, stir it again. If the pigeons only eat this feed slowly, it is advisable to stir the leftovers once or twice between each time they feed on it.

Products administered individually

The **most precise** dosage and **most certain** method of administering medicine is by doing so individually. This does not mean that a certain (guessed) amount of a powdered product should be poured down the pigeon's beak; this would be anything but precise. (This is one of the most common causes of liver damage and death from overdose, and of treatment being too expensive.) To avoid this, powdered products must either by measured out accurately in advance, or more practical factory-encapsulated products must be used.

The great advantage of products **in capsules** is that they contain the exact dose, and so in principle there can be no underdose or overdose. They are easy to use: either we give the pigeon the moistened and thus slippery capsule, or we open it and pour the contents down its beak. (The first is the better of the two solutions.) The encapsulated medicine makes no mess, leaves no remains, does not go off in water, and is certain to reach the pigeon's system. It is the **ideal method** for treating a few birds (e.g. **in a quarantine**), and for this it is the most economical. It has the further benefit that, as well as the main active ingredient, it generally contains many useful additional elements in proportions suitable for pigeons.

Its drawback, on the other hand, is that for a whole flock it is time-consuming to administer, and it disturbs the pigeons on a daily basis (possibly a number of times). When used for a larger number of birds, it is usually more expensive than a product with the same ingredients supplied in a packet for dissolving in drinking water.

*

It is common practice in pigeon-breeding to use certain **human medicines**. Fanciers generally administer these in tablet form to pigeons one by one. If for some reason we are obliged to use such a product, we should without fail ask for a veterinarian's opinion in advance. For we must be aware that **the active ingredient is not the be all and end all**: the nature of the **carrier substance** is also crucial for a medicine's effectiveness. In other words, a medicine designed for human use, even with the same active ingredient, is absorbed from the pigeon's digestive tract differently, if at all, maybe already becoming ruined in the crop, and thus not having its desired effect, as it includes carrier and protection substances which only work in the human body, not in that of a pigeon.

Note

There is a common disadvantage of oral treatments – the agent thus ingested can, for whatever reason, be **disgorged** by the pigeon before it is absorbed. For this reason it is worth observing the birds after treatment, and to substitute any rejected medicine with a new dose.

Injections

Although the majority of active ingredients can be acquired in the form of products administered orally, there are nevertheless instances when the veterinarian opts for treatment by injection. This is the usual method for medicines that are not absorbed from the gut and whose target is not the intestinal canal. Most vaccines also have to be used in the form of injections. This technique has a number of advantages, but also has some drawbacks.

Advantages

Makes precise, individual dosage possible. An injection made in the right place is **certain to be absorbed** – the pigeon cannot disgorge it. Its absorption is **very fast**, and quickly reaches the right level in the bloodstream. It is not dependent on thirst or hunger, and a seriously ill pigeon that can no longer eat or drink is also guaranteed its dose.

Disadvantages

Administering injections is time-consuming and labour intensive, and disturbs the flock. This is particularly true when its application takes place over a number of days. If the person administering the injection is inexperienced, errors can often occur, possibly fatal ones, if the tip of the needle and thus the solution hit a blood vessel. Without regular replacement of the needle – for every single pigeon! – **it can spread infectious disease**.

Products that are inhaled (admitted through breathing)

Many pigeon-owners have tried to administer medicines through vaporization (e.g. tylosin, against respiratory diseases). There is no doubt that this method can successfully be used in industrial-scale poultry husbandry, for example, but it must satisfy certain conditions to be effective. If these are not satisfied, it will not have the desired effect, and may even be detrimental – if for no other reason, then because of the time and money lost on the ineffective treatment.

The essence of the method: using a **specialised** vaporizing apparatus, a spray of fine droplets is formed from the active ingredient solution; the birds breathe in the spray, and thereby the medicine or vaccine.

Advantages

Acts very fast, and even very ill specimens accept their dose. Requires little effort, and does not disturb the flock.

Disadvantages

Requires special apparatus and therefore an investment. Its effectiveness is highly dependent on the humidity level, the temperature and the movement of air. It is only worth administering in a closed space, not outside. It can pollute the surroundings. It can cause respiratory symptoms, and can only be used with a small number of agents.

Dosage

We should always trust the level of the dose of prescription medicines to a veterinarian! Such products are powerful, and the right dose is determined by a number of factors, the calculation of which is not trivial, and requires specialist expertise. If we calculate the dose in an inadequate fashion, we will be lucky to produce a result – and most often we will not be lucky. It is much more likely that we will administer an underdose, which will have no effect, or an overdose, and quite simply poison the flock.

The situation is different if we purchase an OTC product. We can ask for the veterinarian's advice here, too, but we can also simply follow the instructions on the packaging.

One of the most common mistakes in measuring out medicines is the misconception that the effect of the medicine is directly proportional to the dose administered, i.e. that if we give three times the dose prescribed, we can expect three times stronger an effect. Quite the opposite is true. The majority of medicines **influence the system as a foreign substance**, which the body has to battle against. It is pointless to give multiple doses of antibiotics, for example – this is not only a waste of money, but is also harmful to the pigeon. In the end, it is the pigeon's immune system which defeats the pathogen; the antibiotics are but a help in this. An exaggerated amount is just an extra burden for the body. Often it is exactly this burden that proves too much for the system to bear.

A lesson from personal experience: a breeder friend of mine once told me how valiantly he had dealt with one of his pigeons having a cold – for a week he pushed two doxycycline capsules a day down its throat. The medicine in question is for humans, its prescribed dose one capsule every 24 hours for an adult. It is not difficult to calculate that my friend had administered about 200 times too much of the medicine. The cold was indeed dispensed with, but so too was the pigeon, which passed away soon after the successful cure – most probably, its liver could not take the generous treatment.

*

Fanciers most often administer medicine and curative products mixed in drinking water. In this case, doses can be calculated in two different ways:

- relative to amount of drinking water consumed per day

- relative to the pigeons' body mass (body weight)

Dosage measured relative to quantity of drinking water

For powder-based products, dosage is marked as grams per x litres of drinking water; for fluid-based products, in millilitres per x litres. A gram of powder is roughly equivalent to a level coffee-spoon; it is best to measure out fluids using a plastic syringe. For units of measure and conversion data, see Table 1. (*You can find the tablets at the very end of the book.)*

The amount of medicine needed per litre of drinking water is easy to measure and can be administered precisely, but this method has its disadvantages, indeed **dangers**. In extreme heat or during breeding season the consumption of water increases, often significantly. If we follow the same proportions per litre, it is easy to see that on a hot day, drinking twice as much water, the birds will accept twice as much of the medicine, thus overdosing on it. In the case of certain drugs absorbed from the gut, this can be outrightly dangerous, and the pigeons can be poisoned. It happens particularly when administering dimetridazole that pigeons drinking too much medicated water display signs of poisoning, and in extreme cases even die of it.

To avoid this, we should follow this procedure (unless the veterinarian specifically instructs otherwise!). When measuring out the dose proportional to an amount of drinking water, **we should take the average daily water consumption as our reference point**, and use this to work out the dose! (*For a detailed example, see the section entitled "Canker – Trichomoniasis".*)

The other disadvantage of putting medicines in water is that unless we use suitable drinkers, the pigeons will splash out the medicated water, thus wasting it, which is a rather expensive luxury, not to mention the fact that they will consume less of the active ingredient. The use of specialized pigeon drinkers is also advisable because the water becomes less dirty in them, and there is also less loss from evaporation. (The latter can cause medicated water to become too concentrated.)

Dosage measured relative to body weight

As the level of water consumption can vary greatly, often a calculation relative to body mass (body weight) can allow a more precise dosage. For many products, the dose is only specified in this form. For this we calculate the total weight of the flock as a whole, by multiplying the average weight by the total number of birds. The average weight can be established with an estimate, but we are given a more precise figure if we weigh a few pigeons that appear average. With an accurate determination of the total weight of the flock we can avoid the common problem of overdosing and underdosing. Underdosing can cause ineffectiveness; overdosing to serious side-effects, apart from being wasteful and damaging to the environment.

If at all possible, we should always use products specifically designed for pigeons! But there are occasions when the necessary agent does not appear in any specialized pigeon medicine, and so we have no option but to use other medicines, e.g. ones designed for chickens. In this case, there is naturally no dosage for pigeons on the packaging, but the specified measure for chickens provides a point of reference. We should avoid the traps presented by adopting this dosage directly.

The dosage of most medicines should really be calculated in proportion to **body surface area** rather than body weight, because this is **much more precise**. The surface of the body is what separates the bird and the outside world, through which the bird is penetrated and through which it releases many substances; in short, it is the point of continuous contact with its surroundings. Measurement of dosage relative to body surface area is almost impossible, however, as it is very hard to calculate, even to guess, what this area is. (We note that certain human medicines that are powerful and require highly accurate dosage are calculated and administered with this method.) Thus in the case of pigeons it is the body weight that we take into account – the only problem being that **body weight is not proportionate to body surface area**, and so **adapting the dosage for chickens can lead to mistakes**.

Let us take a perfect example! If we compare a cube with edges of 2cm with one of 1cm, we immediately see that the mass of the larger cube is eight times that of the smaller one, but its complete surface area only four times greater: the surface area increases less than the weight does. The same is true in reverse: if we decrease the weight, the surface area declines to a smaller degree. From this it follows that **smaller bodies have a larger surface area relative to their weight**. This is why young birds lose heat faster than adult ones: the smaller amount of heat generated by the smaller body is released into the surroundings through a surface that is relatively larger. It can withstand strong heat better for the same reason: relatively speaking, the area for it to release the heat is larger. We can also deduce from their relatively large body surface area that the young must expend more energy on producing feathers, and that there is a larger terrain for parasites to attack them.

So, if the mass of a half-kilo pigeon is half that of a one-kilo chicken, its body surface area is not half, but more, about two-thirds. If the pigeon weighs a quarter of a kilo, the weight-surface area ratio is even further distorted: e.g. **the total surface area of four ¼ kilo pigeons, i.e. "a kilo" of pigeons, is approximately double that of a one kilo chicken**.

The logical consequence of the above would be that the treatment of pigeons requires double the dose of that of chickens. This only a generalization, however, as with some agents we must not increase the dose. We should always discuss dosage with the veterinarian, lest we poison the whole flock, or spend money unnecessarily. In general, the advice would be that if the dosage for chickens is prescribed within a certain range, then for pigeons we should use the highest dosage allowed. For example, if the prescribed dosage for chickens is 10-20mg per kilogram of body weight, in the case of pigeons we should administer 20mg.

Time of day and duration of application

In this book, we examine the time of treatment from two angles:

- the number and time of treatments on a given day

- the length of the treatment programme as a whole
(the number of days treatment occurs)

Treatments on a given day

Different medicines are absorbed into and released from the body at different speeds. Sometimes two agents are absorbed at the same pace but one is released slowly and the other fast. That is, different drugs maintain the **efficient level in the bloodstream for different lengths of time**. It is with all these in mind that we should determine the daily schedule for treatment, paying due attention to circumstances like the current temperature, the method of application, the time of year, the breeding-season, possible parallel treatments, etc.

The daily programme of treatment depends on a number of factors; it is the veterinarian's task to determine it, and the fancier's to keep to it. In general, the key question is how many times the medicine should be administered per day. There are agents (e.g. doxycycline) that only need to be given once a day, because they are quickly absorbed and maintain an efficient level in the bloodstream for 24 hours afterwards. Other agents (e.g. penicillin derivatives) are released within hours, and thus need to be administered two or three times a day, or even continuously.

Kick-therapy

We call a daily or twice-daily dose kick-therapy. The essence of this is that the daily dosage is measured out in one part (morning **or** evening) or in two parts (morning **and** evening), mixed into a relatively small quantity of water, just enough for the pigeons to drink it quickly. Once this has succeeded, we give them plain water (or other agents, e.g. vitamins) for the rest of the day.

Administering liquids continuously

Medicines that are quick to be released must generally be administered on a continuous basis. Here we should strive to estimate the amount of water to be consumed that day as accurately as possible, and take this into account when determining the amount of the agent to be added to each litre of drinking water. In the course of this kind of treatment, pigeons cannot be given plain water or bathing water.

Warning! **In hot weather** drinking water consumed can increase multifold. On such occasions, if we need to administer liquids continuously, **we cannot always give medicated water of the same consistency**, because like this the consumption of medicine would multiply in the same way! This is uneconomical and bad for the birds' health. We should decrease the concentration per litre to compensate, e.g. if twice as much water is consumed, we should add half as much medicine per litre. An even better answer is if we administer the daily dose, based on **average** daily water consumption or on body weight, in a number of parts: at least three, but ideally four (in a small amount of water, kick-therapy fashion), providing plain water in the periods between treatment, if necessary (in hot weather).

Note

The composition and the carrier substance of medicines in capsules are generally designed to make a single daily application possible. This should take place roughly every 24 hours, i.e. every morning or every evening.

The duration of the treatment as a whole

Different products are administered for very different periods of time. Some on a single occasion (e.g. vaccines, deworming agents), some for a few days or weeks (vitamins, antibiotics), still others on an almost continuous basis (food supplements). Vitamins and substances administered over a longer period can be given every day, every other day, or for example every day for one week, then a week's break, and so on. The length of the treatment depends on a number of factors, which we will deal with in the respective chapter. Here we will look at one of the most important of these.

Unfortunately, experience across the world suggests that more and more antibiotics that until recently worked well have declined in their effectiveness, or have lost their power over the pathogens in question altogether. We refer to the "immunity" of bacteria against specific antibiotics as **medicine resistance**, which means that the antibiotic has no effect on the bacterium strain in question. This resistance is genetic, and so bacteria evolving from this strain will also be resistant to the antibiotic. Just to make things even more complicated, there also exists so-called **cross-resistance**, which means that the resistance of a given strain of bacteria automatically extends to other antibiotics that are similar in structure.

There is also natural resistance, when a particular antibiotic has no effect on a given type of bacterium, e.g. penicillin derivatives are powerless with mycoplasms. Far more significant from our point of view is **acquired resistance**, when a particular strain of bacteria **becomes immune** to an antibiotic that was previously effective.

It is primarily **we who evoke the development of acquired resistance** when **we administer the antibiotic for the wrong length of time**. (With a hint of irony, we could equally say that it has taken arduous and tiring "breeding" work to develop strains of bacteria capable of scoffing at all or almost all antibiotics. This is true for humans, too: "I'll knock back a couple of amoxicillins, good for my cold".) Antibiotic treatment lasting for just a day or two does not remove all the pathogens from the system, but **amongst the bacteria that survive the proportion of resistant ones increases**. For the medicine has no effect on them, and they merrily continue to multiply, while the medicine is effective against the others, and so the proportion of non-resistant bacteria is reduced. And if the treatment is brief, these **susceptible ones only decline in number**, they do not all disappear, and so the immune system cannot turn its full attention to the resistant ones: its power is divided, it becomes exhausted prematurely, and thus recovery is not complete, and the pigeon continues to be a carrier of bacteria. As the "immunity" of the resistant bacteria enjoying increasing dominance in the bird's system is passed on to their descendants, it follows that **with each new treatment of**

inadequate duration, the proportion of bacteria which are resistant to the medicine increases – and thus, sooner or later, the whole strain will become resistant.

The development of similarly resistant strains can also result **if the dose of the antibiotic used is smaller than required**, that is, **in the case of an underdose**.

If a resistant strain infects another pigeon or flock, **it is too late to use the antibiotic in question, even if for a prolonged period**. As the number of antibiotics is limited, and bacterium strains are capable of developing multiple resistance (i.e. resistance to more than one antibiotic), strains have emerged over the years that are not affected by any antibiotic currently in use!

It is highly important, therefore, that we continuously administer the antibiotic in the prescribed dose and for the prescribed period. The correct duration of treatment varies enormously, however, depending on the disease and the antibiotic used.

In general, we can say that **the minimum period for antibiotic treatment is three (consecutive!) days.** This is true even if we are only using the medicine in a "preventive" fashion (to destroy bacteria lurking in the bird's system to prevent them spreading later on).

In this day and age, however, a three-day treatment is usually not enough. For **salmonellas at least a week** is recommended, but many advise a continuous course of **10-14 days**. In the case of **ornithosis** caused by chlamydias, an even longer period of treatment may be required, **as long as thirty days**!

*

Note

Without digging too much into the mystery of genetics, it is worth mentioning that the resistance of each bacterium is a result of **random** mutation (or conjugation, or a bacteriophage bearing the resistance gene). On the one hand, the chance of evolvement of a resistant microorganism is very low; on the other hand, it is not influenced by us (and the medication that we use). We are, however, responsible if with the incorrect use of antibiotics **we help the proliferation of these bacteria**, which are otherwise only present in small numbers in the system, **and the resistant strains that develop thus spread in the outside world**.

*

The resistance of bacteria is causing increasingly significant problems in **public health**, and sadly the number of deaths caused by multiresistant bacterial strains is becoming higher and higher. On the veterinary side, we can help our colleagues in human health care – and of course everyone else – by giving preference to those types of antibiotics (antibacterial agents) that are exclusively for use in animal health care. Examples of such drugs not used in the human sector are **apramycin, tylosin, flumequin** and **enrofloxacin**.

3. Medicine inside the body

We only discuss the path and effect of medicines in the system briefly and from a practical point of view.

Absorption

Most medicines for internal use, however they are administered (by mouth, injection, spraying), have to be absorbed from the point at which this occurs, i.e. have to travel further in order to reach the appropriate organ or organs. There are clear differences in the way the various active ingredients are absorbed, and to ignore these can cause treatment to be unsuccessful.

Absorption from the intestinal system

Most often, we treat the flock by mouth. Different drugs behave differently in the intestinal canal, or are absorbed from it in different ways.

Of the various **vitamins**, **vitamins soluble in fat** (vitamins A, D, E and K) can only be absorbed from the intestinal canal if there is enough grease in the food consumed simultaneously with them. The seeds of cereals contain vegetable oil in adequate quantities, and so we only have to see that pigeons have enough feed during the course of vitamins. If for some reason this does not happen – e.g. due to illness – we should be aware that a fat-soluble vitamin provided in drinking water, though drunk by the pigeons, will not be absorbed adequately and thus will not be effective. When a pigeon has not eaten for days, it is preferable to provide fat-soluble vitamins in injected form.

Antibiotics given by mouth are absorbed from the alimentary canal **in varying quantities**. The absorption of certain agents is affected by how full the intestinal canal is, e.g. ampicillin, while for others, like amoxicillin, it is not.

Although we will return to this when discussing each separate agent, we will now list those antibiotics administered by mouth but which are not absorbed from the gut. We do this because even professionals can commit the error, for example, of trying to treat respiratory illness with antibiotics administered by mouth but not getting any further than the intestines. If given by mouth, we can only expect such drugs to have an effect in the intestinal canal itself; if the pathogens also attack other organs (respiratory passages, joints, etc.), the drug will not reach them.

The following antibiotics are hardly absorbed from the intestinal canal, if at all: **neomycin, streptomycin, colistin, gentamycin, spectinomycin**.

The fact that certain antibiotics are not absorbed from the intestines can be advantageous. If we only want to treat enteritis, it is advisable to choose from among agents that are not absorbed, for by staying in the intestinal tract **these put the lightest burden on the bird's system**.

The absorption of the active ingredients from the intestinal canal affected by many factors. The **pH value of the intestinal contents** is not insignificant, e.g. in the case of tetracyclines, especially doxycycline. If we get the flock to drink doxycycline, we should always introduce organic acid to the medicated drinking water – the easiest being apple vinegar or a ready-made acid mixture. Doxycycline is much more readily absorbed from an acidic environment than from an alkaline one.

In the case of **intestinal inflammation**, the penetrability of the intestinal wall is altered, which can equally cause increased or decreased absorption. If the intestinal inflammation is accompanied by **diarrhoea**, the increased rate of excretion of faeces means that the intestinal contents leave the system faster than expected, resulting in decreased absorption of the medicine. For this reason, if the diarrhoea is severe, it may be necessary to complement the treatment with injections.

Absorption of injected drugs

Unless we commit some vaccination error, the agent in an injection given below the skin or in a muscle is generally absorbed quickly. An expertly performed injection is more certain to be effective than a product given by mouth. It has the following drawbacks, however:

- risks associated with injections (damage to certain muscle groups; embolism)

- laborious and time-consuming if applied to the whole flock

- disturbs the specimen and the flock

- the needle can transfer infection (if not changed)

Despite these disadvantages, in many cases, e.g. when using immunizing vaccines, we have no choice but to use an injection. It is a common complaint that after vaccination the location of the injection become "knotted", a change which does not disappear of its own accord. This is particularly observable in the case of oil-based vaccines, if the substance is not administered deep enough (if it was injected into the skin, not the tissue underneath it). Another cause can be the use of a vaccine that is too cold, or failing gently to massage the point of injection. If we identify such a protrusion a few days after the injection, we can usually eliminate it with the local application of creams causing hyperaemia (camphoric or mentholated substances), and it is absorbed without trace.

*

Many agents are absorbed through the skin if applied to it **externally**. There are products available (e.g. certain substances against parasites) that must be dripped onto the skin. The active ingredient spreads over the surface of the skin and/or is absorbed through it, and once in the bloodstream exerts its effect throughout the body.

Transdermal absorption has its dangers, however. Some products attacking parasites cannot be used on pigeons, because if absorbed through the skin, the active agent causes poisoning, or even death. These substances can be absorbed through a person's skin in the same way, and so we should always use protective materials (rubber gloves, face mask), if, for example, we are spraying an empty cage with such products!

The mechanism of action

There are a wide variety of ways in which the different agents achieve their real effect on the system or the pathogens preying on it. Even a mere list of these is beyond the scope of this book; here we simply note that if we use a drug against the pathogens attacking the body, we must be prepared, alongside the desired action (e.g. killing bacteria), for a number of side-effects, because once inside the bird's system a medicine also affects the system itself. (Indeed – staying with the same example – the antibiotic will also have an adverse effect on the normal intestinal bacteria in the body.)

The same is also true in reverse: if we treat the system itself, the substance given (e.g. a vitamin) also has an effect on the living creatures in the body, whether harmful or benevolent; this effect is often significant and not to be ignored. (E.g. when administering vitamin B1, we are also "doing good" to the coccidia pathogens.)

We should always weigh up the expected effect before beginning a course of treatment: **the extent of the hoped benefit from the medication must be compared with the extent of the damage from its anticipated side-effects**, and it is in the light of this that we should decide whether or not to opt for the treatment.

Metabolism

After a certain time in the system, a **foreign substance** (e.g. antibiotic or deworming agent) is transformed, and, after exerting its effect (or not, in a less fortunate case), it disintegrates. This occurs because the majority of medicines that enter the body act as substances foreign to it, that is **as poisons**, and so the system strives to rid itself of them: it transforms them and breaks them up in order to render them ineffective and so it can release them altogether.

We should give credence to the saying: **a little of it and it is medicine, a lot of it and it is poison**. It is not only wasteful to give medicines in larger quantities than those prescribed, it is directly harmful: by doing so we create an unnecessary burden on a system already weakened by illness.

Even the majority of **beneficial** vitamins, amino acids and **minerals** have to be transformed by the system for them to be utilized. This conversion process requires effort, and so an overdose of the otherwise beneficial substance puts an unnecessary extra burden on the bird's system. At best, any overdose of the medicine is not absorbed from the gut, and the body releases it unaltered; in this case we have "only" wasted money and polluted the environment. In a worse instance, the system is forced to perform extra effort to rid itself of the unnecessary and dangerous burden of the excess material. At worst, the body is incapable of releasing the substance in time, and this causes illness.

Elimination

The unused or disintegrated agent is removed from the system in a number of different ways. The liver, kidneys and lungs all participate in its excretion, but a huge amount of it is discharged through the skin. Here we are most interested in one particular form of excretion, that which takes place via crop milk.

During rearing, pigeons feed their young with crop milk, the composition of which is greatly influenced by the feed and medication consumed by the parent at the time. Medicine introduced by mouth can directly return to the outside world, or rather the system of the youngster, through crop milk, but this crop milk also contains other components. Active secretion takes place through the wall of the crop or the intestines: substances return from the system to the cavity of the intestinal canal. In this way **the youngster can even partake in medicines which its parent received not by mouth but in the form of an injection!**

4. Drug interactions

We know that in developed countries there are many thousands of veterinary medicines in circulation, as well as many health care products that can legally be distributed but do not qualify as medicines. Among these, there are many hundreds of products suitable for pigeons.

These products can – on the basis of a suitable diagnosis, of course – safely be used to treat pigeons. There will often be occasions, however, when we wish to treat our flock with a number of products at once, or directly after one another. In such instances we must be clear which medicines can and which cannot be mixed with one another. Administering wrongly chosen medicines in parallel can lessen or nullify the effectiveness of some medicines, or even have damaging consequences and cause harmful substances to appear.

If are to take just a hundred different medicines as our base and choose two of them to administer, there are five thousand possible variations; if we choose three at once, there are already **hundreds of thousands of variations**. It goes without saying that of these many combinations will be incorrect, where the two or three different agents "clash" with each other. No one can memorize so many variations, and so the issue of whether medicines can be mixed or administered simultaneously must always be decided on a case-by-case basis. Furthermore, many products are mixtures to begin with, that is they contain more than one active ingredient, which makes things even more complicated. As does the fact that certain medicines cannot be given immediately after one another, but only after a certain amount of time has passed.

Medicines administered at once (mixed) can begin to interact even **before entry into the system**; in general, this means they will be ruined. It is much more common for medicines or their effects to influence each other **once inside the system**, which can seriously affect the success of the treatment – whether in a negative or positive fashion.

Interaction outside the body

We will often learn that two medicines "clash" chemically even before they are applied. When dissolving the medicines in water, for example, the solution will become cloudy, flakes will emerge from it, or it will be a strange colour. The two medicines react in the water solution, and various salts or other compounds are formed, with results visible to the naked eye. It is almost certain that one or more of the mixed agents is ruined. We now know that these medicines should not be mixed.

Mixability appears in the official descriptions of registered medicines, and the veterinarian should pay heed. For example, he can prescribe that a vitamin product be added to the drinking water when dissolving an antibiotic. Naturally, he will prescribe or recommend products that are mixable, products which under normal conditions can be poured into the same water. But there are exceptions. Such an exception is if **the drinking water is overly ferrous or too cold**. This can mean that otherwise highly compatible medicines clash after all. If we suspect such a problem, it is best if we perform a mixing test, to prevent greater financial loss. We put the medicines in a decilitre of drinking water, in a proportionate dose, then mix them up well. If they dissolve fully, and we see no flaking or lasting cloudiness, then there is no reason not to mix up the full amount.

Important! If when mixing the various products there is no visible alteration to the aqueous solution, this is no guarantee that the active ingredients have not bonded with or damaged each other. Therefore we should always be careful when mixing products, and take professional advice!

*

A number of soluble products designed for pigeons **have multiple components to begin with**, with some having ten or more active ingredients. Medicines this complicated should not be mixed with other products – unless the veterinarian directs otherwise – because it is almost certain that we will damage at least one of their components in the process!

Interaction inside the body

Whether we use medicines simultaneously or directly after one another, they will meet inside the pigeon's system, and most probably **have an effect on one another**. From the body's point of view, this effect can be **beneficial**, if the agents strengthen each other, as in the case of certain combinations of antibiotics. This interaction can be **insignificant** for the body, but it can also be **harmful**. The latter is true of certain antibiotics, for example: if inside the body at the same time, they can drain each other's effect.

The issue of medicinal interaction in the system is a specialist one for veterinary science, one whose understanding requires professional expertise. Here I would merely like to draw attention to **a few errors often committed in practice**.

Many breeders make the mistake of continuing or finishing the course of antibiotics with a different antibiotic of their own choosing (e.g. one left over from before). This is wrong for a number of reasons. From the point of view of interaction between medicines, it is wrong because **antibiotics inhibit each other's effect more often than they augment it**. A bacteriostatic and a bactericidal antibiotic generally weaken each other, and so will be much less effective if administered together than separately – the result will be the opposite of the one expected, deterioration instead of improvement. Not to mention the fact that such botched treatment leads directly to the development of medicine resistance.

Another serious error is **the use of antibiotics during certain vaccinations**, or immediately before or after them. A badly-timed dose of antibiotics can ruin the active ingredient of the vaccine, so preventing it from having its protective effect – something we will only wake up to when the illness appears.

Gentamycin is a typical antibiotic that can enter into countless unwanted reactions with other agents. During its use, and for a few days afterwards, the pigeon must not be given any other antibiotic (with the exception of amoxicillin and lincomycin), nor vitamin C, nor vitamins belonging to the B group, for these can react detrimentally in the system with the gentamycin (still) present there!

A few products against coccidiosis contain **amprolium**. The latter destroys the coccidia by excluding vitamin B1, which these parasites need to survive. So we are committing an error if we give pigeons a mixture including vitamin B1 in their water during or immediately after treatment with amprolium, for by doing so we decrease or nullify its effect on the coccidia.

A common error is providing **probiotics** in pigeons' drinking water simultaneously with antibiotics. The beneficial bacteria emerging and propagating from the germinating probiotic are destroyed as a result of the antibiotic, and also "use up" much of the latter, leaving less of the active ingredient to attack the pathogens. For this reason we should not administer probiotics during courses of antibiotics of a week or less – only afterwards, over a period of five days. In the course of longer antibiotic treatment for many weeks (ornithosis), however, it may be necessary to administer probiotics in the meantime, depending on the type of antibiotic, or rather on its effect on the normal intestinal flora. This should be decided by the veterinarian during the treatment, based on the results of tests on bacterial cultures. In general it is advisable on such occasions to choose antibiotics that are **less damaging to the intestinal flora**. To continue the example of ornithosis: oxytetracycline, chlortetracycline and doxycycline all (in principle) have an effect on chlamydias, but of these it is doxycycline that damages normal intestinal bacteria the least. (It is also the least toxic, another reason to prefer it when administering medicine over a longer period.)

III. Diseases by group

Contagious diseases

1. Bacteria-induced diseases

About bacteria in general

Bacteria are single-cell creatures that are invisible to the naked eye. Their size varies from 0.1 to 10 microns (1 millimetre =

1,000 microns). Their structure varies from the simple to the complicated – for example, some do not even have a cell wall. For our purposes, we distinguish **beneficial** and **pathogenic** bacteria, though this classification is arbitrary and not necessarily precise. For example, some types of bacteria are largely beneficial or neutral for pigeons, but in certain conditions can still become pathogens.

Unlike viruses, bacteria are capable of independent reproduction, and **boast their own metabolism**. **From this it follows that certain poisons (antibiotics) will have an effect on them**. Antibiotics either destroy them or stop them from proliferating. The former are bactericidal, or bacterium killers; the latter are bacteriostatics.

Bacteria reproduce, or rather multiply, by fission. They do this very quickly: in the right circumstances, an ordinary coli intestinal bacterium starts to divide almost immediately, doubling its numbers every quarter of an hour(!). For example, if a single cell starts proliferating at midnight, by midnight the following day the number of its daughter cells will, in theory, be 2 to the power of 96, an extraordinary sum.

It is impossible even to imagine such a number – let us consider this in slightly greater detail! If the size of a bacterium is a thousandth of a millimetre, then a colony of around a billion bacteria represents a mass the size of a pinhead. Let's conduct an imaginary experiment. We take a coli bacterium, place it in a culture medium at 37 degrees Celsius for it to proliferate. As the coli bacterium is capable of splitting, that is doubling, every quarter of an hour, in half an hour one bacterium will be four, and in an hour will be sixteen. In two hours we will have 256 specimens. If they continue to proliferate at the same rate, in the thirtieth quarter of an hour, that is seven and a half hours later, there will be about a billion bacteria, about as many as fit in a space the size of a pinhead.

After this – at least according to the laws of mathematics – all hell breaks loose. After the fiftieth round of splitting, the culture would be a litre in volume; fifteen hours from the outset, it would fill a cubic metre! And if this fantastic pace continues, the mass of bacteria by the end of the twenty-fourth hour would be eighty billion cubic metres, roughly the size of Mount Everest. All of this in the space of a single day, from a single bacterium! These numbers are only theoretical, of course, but adequate to give us a feeling of **how dangerous an enemy** superior creatures have to battle with day by day.

Fortunately, there are a number of defence mechanisms which stop this furious multiplication at a much earlier stage. The body protects itself, takes up the struggle with the intruders, destroys them and weakens them – if its immune system is in order, of course. The orgy of the bacteria is also limited by other factors. As their numbers increase, so their nutrition becomes less and less sufficient. The amount of their own metabolic by-products grows, which has a toxic "backfire" effect on them after a certain concentration is reached. (Humans do the same – we call it industrial pollution.) As a matter of interest, we note that laboratory experiments have shown that if the best conditions are provided for the bacteria – if there is an unlimited supply of nutrition and poisonous metabolic by-products are removed on a continuous basis – the speed of proliferation declines once a certain density is reached, then soon stops altogether. We do not know the real explanation for this phenomenon: it seems that after a while, bacteria, like other creatures, have simply had enough of each other. In any case, it is the fantastic self-regulatory power of nature that is behind this.

Bacterial cultures

As bacteria have their own metabolism, and multiply quickly, **it is relatively easy to cultivate them in artificial conditions**. We call this method "culturing". In our case, in sterile conditions, we take a sample from the (living or dead) pigeon to be examined, from its various excretions (e.g. faeces, tears, saliva) or its organs, and spread this sample onto a gelatin-like culture medium in a Petri dish (a special cell culture plate), which is maintained at a stable temperature of 37 degrees Celsius. In the right conditions, the sample bacteria begin to split, and, depending on their type, may within 8-12 hours form colonies that are visible to the eye. On the one hand, with this method we can identify the **types of bacteria** to be found in the sample, and thus in the pigeon's body; on the other hand, by using antibiotic reagents, we can also find out **exactly which antibiotics the strains of bacteria are responsive to**, and which they have become resistant to.

Culturing is thus a very useful technique, which helps prevent the evolution of medicine-resistant bacterium strains, and which also **saves huge amounts of time and money** by avoiding blindly-administered and ineffective doses of antibiotics. How often it has turned out that the most expensive antibiotic treatment, the "best weapon in our armoury", has proved to be useless, while an entirely different, much cheaper active ingredient, determined by bacterial cultures, has happened to be the best choice!

Naturally there are **limitations** to this approach. Firstly, the sample must be fresh and clean. It must not be contaminated as the sample is taken, else it will be the bacteria in the outside world that will grow, squeezing out the pathogens under investigation. In the same way, culturing cannot give a diagnostically valuable result from a pigeon that has died, but not recently. Unfortunately mycoplasma grows very slowly, giving results only after 10-12 days, by which time it is usually too late. The culturing of chlamydias is also difficult and time consuming, requiring special laboratory equipment. Thus the bacteriological testing of these pathogens is not routine. It is very important to note that the bacterium causing the most problems in pigeon-breeding, salmonella, **can be cultured easily and quickly**, and so bacteriological testing of a pigeon or flock suffering from paratyphoid is highly recommended. Furthermore, as a form of verification, it can quickly be repeated during or following the treatment. **Coli** bacteria and cocci are also quick and easy to culture.

In these instances, however, bacteriological lab tests **can produce misleading results**. The sample normally consists of one or two pigeons (whether alive or dead), and thus there is always the possibility that the culture we grow is not representative of the flock as a whole – i.e. that we identify a strain other than the one giving the flock the most problems. This can happen because the specimen from which the sample was taken happens (also) to be suffering from a different illness.

Much more common are cases in which there are a number of strains of salmonella in a flock with paratyphoid, for example, and where these strains vary in their resistance to antibiotics. So if we identify a single strain and select antibiotics on the basis of it, the treatment may be unsuccessful for pigeons infected with different strains. (Some of the pigeons are cured, while the remainder are not.) It is for these reasons that the result of bacterial culturing must only be evaluated and used while bearing all the other circumstances in mind.

Important!

It is worth mentioning **one special advantage** of using bacterial cultures. If the sample is taken from droppings, the beneficial residents of the intestine grow in addition to the pathogenic bacterial strains. The antibiotics being examined have an effect on them, too, and so we will be able to see **which antibiotics cause the least damage to the normal (beneficial) intestinal bacteria**. This allows us to choose antibiotics for the treatment which are effective in destroying the harmful bacteria, but spare the helpful bacteria in the intestines. As one of the most serious side-effects of antibiotics is the destruction of normal intestinal flora, avoiding this can contribute greatly to the success of treatment!

*

We can use various chemical compounds (poisons) to defend against pathogenic bacteria once they have entered the body and their excessive proliferation is threatening its well-being. This includes the group of antibiotics, which is growing in size as it decreases in effectiveness. We do have other chemicals, like copper sulphate or potassium permanganate, but they are slowly becoming forgotten. We can use plant extracts like the alkaloids of garlic. These substances affect bacteria directly just as antibiotics do, killing them or preventing their proliferation. But we should never forget that in the end **it is the body's immune system that defeats the pathogen** – substances (medicines) introduced from outside are just a help in this.

***

In the following, we look at the most important bacterium-induced illnesses in pigeons. We characterize the various pathogens, their mode of infection, the damage they inflict on the body, the symptoms they induce, as well as possibilities for fighting them.

Paratyphoid

Paratyphoid, caused by salmonellas, is one of the illnesses in pigeons that is most common, most difficult to contain, and most harmful, and which can lead to a large rate of deaths. The pathogen can also infect humans.

Salmonellas are widespread bacteria all over the world. There are seven subspecies, and a large number of types belonging to them. At present we are aware of about 2100 different types(!). In pigeons it is Salmonella typhimurium var. Copenhagen that occurs most often, but many other salmonella variants can also cause illness.

Although strong disinfectants have a good effect on them, from an epidemiological point of view salmonellas are highly resistant bacteria: they are capable of remaining virulent for many years in the body and even for a year or 18 months outside, if the conditions are favourable.

Transmission

Salmonellas are capable of spreading from one bird to another in a great variety of ways, whether by direct contact or indirectly.

Most often it is via the droppings of pigeons (or wild birds) carrying the salmonellas that the loft becomes infected. It is very important for us to know that **a seemingly healthy pigeon can be a carrier of salmonellas**, possibly **shedding the pathogens** and infecting its surroundings for years or a lifetime. Symptom-free carriage is generally limited to the gut, which is where salmonellas hide and reproduce, and from where they are continuously released into the outside world.

Under certain conditions, the release of salmonellas **increases**. In the event of massive **coccidiosis**, for example, there are many more salmonellas to be found in a bird's faeces. The situation is similar when the amount of **feed consumed** decreases. The most probable explanation for this is that the nutrition for normal intestinal bacteria is insufficient, and so the level of their acidic metabolic by-products, which are beneficial to the host, declines. Consequently, a more alkaline environment in the gut is highly favourable for the proliferation of the salmonellas. In the event of persistent stress (e.g. transportation, shows, hot weather), consumption of feed decreases, and pathogens can easily lodge themselves and proliferate in the birds' vulnerable bodies.

Salmonellas can also spread as a result of infected feed. The feed can be infected by other animals, e.g. mice, rats, or lice. The pathogen also infects by inhalation, entering the susceptible bird by clinging to bits of dust in the air (e.g. emanating from dried and pulverized faeces).

A typical and common mode by which salmonellas spread is related to pigeons' **breeding**. The parents infect each other when mating, and in theory the infection of the young can take place at any time. The bacterium can enter the **ovary** itself, and thus the **egg** comes into the world already infected, but the eggshell can also become infected in the cloaca when being laid, or in the nest once outside. The nestling can also be infected during the rearing period, through crop milk.

What with the large number of sources of infection, and the high survival potential of the pathogen, there are hardly any lofts which are not infected with salmonella. The illness often breaks out in an infected loft **towards the end of the rearing period**, because by this time **the immune system of the parents becomes exhausted**, and the dormant salmonellas begin to multiply within their bodies. On such occasions not just the parent becomes ill, but – as it releases the pathogen in great quantities – it massively infects its environment, thus passing the disease on to other pigeons (or even to other types of birds kept near the loft, e.g. chickens!).

The pathogen can also be spread through saliva, when the pigeon carrying it infects drinking water, passing on the illness to the other pigeons. Given that salmonellas are capable of proliferating in water, this is a very significant source of danger.

Damage

The bacteria most often infect by mouth, and the first symptoms are often associated with illness of the **digestive canal**. From here the salmonellas cheerfully break through into the bloodstream, and, scattered throughout the system, attach themselves to the widest variety of organs. The symptoms vary strongly, depending on the organ attacked.

Symptoms

Typically symptoms develop according to **age-group**.

An **embryo** that is infected early (while still in the body of the hen) usually dies, and the egg blackens, becoming rotten. If the infection is not serious or happens during incubation, the infected chick starts pipping, but on most occasions it perishes **in the course of hatching**. Even if it does manage to hatch, it will not live for more than **a few days**. The majority of such youngsters die from diarrhoea (dehydration).

In **young pigeons** symptoms occur most often in **acute** form. Severe **diarrhoea** develops, which is mucous-gelatinous, and a greener shade of white. We may find tiny gas bubbles in the faeces, which in the case of serious intestinal inflammation can even be sanguineous. The young either die quickly, or, if the illness is more protracted, their growth is retarded and they become very thin. It is typical for only one of the youngsters in a particular nest to become ill or perish, and for the other to remain healthy.

As, like paramyxovirus, salmonella attacks the central nervous system, **neurological symptoms** and incoordination can develop. These can cause abnormal posture or movement of the neck, accompanied by head tremors.

The bacteria **can attack the lungs, liver, kidneys and other internal organs, as well as the skeletal muscles**. Necrotic, lardaceously gleaming areas develop in the organs. If the necrotic area is large enough, it represents a direct threat to the operation of the organ and thus to the pigeon's life. Organs thus constrained in their operation display their characteristic symptoms, which can be very diverse.

The **chronic form** occurs more in the **older** age-group. Diarrhoea is less severe or not present, while swelling of **joints**, particularly the elbow joint, is common. One or more joints are painful or swollen to some degree; the pigeon lets its wing droop, and can also become limp. Incoordination can also emerge. Necrotic areas can be found in internal organs, though their size is less than in the acute form. Necrotic plexuses often develop in the skeletal muscles. The effect on breast muscles can cause a prolonged, usually permanent decline in **flying performance**. Another typical effect is the pigeon losing body weight or "going light".

The appearance of these symptoms is often very **varied**. The males are more sensitive than the hens: even as adults they are more likely to fall ill with acute symptoms, and a large proportion of them perish within a day or two. The hens appear more resistant – in their case it is the chronic arthritic form that is more common.

*

Paratyphoid illness must be **differentiated from**:

- **paramyxoviral illness**: because of nervous symptoms, head tremors, twisted neck
- **adenovirus**: because of the fast death of youngsters
- **coccidiosis**: because of occasional bloody diarrhoea
- **intestinal worms**: because of weight loss, emaciation, chronic diarrhoea, stunted development
- **canker**: because of early death of the young
- **coli**: because of swelling of joints, embryo death, and infertility
- **ornithosis**: because of diarrhoea, sometimes greenish, and sudden death of chicks
- **poisons**: because of neurological symptoms (incoordination, quivering) and sudden deaths

Treatment

There are three principles we should bear in mind when treating paratyphoid:

- we must perform **targeted** antibiotic treatment
- we must treat the **whole flock**
- the period of the treatment must be **at least 7 but ideally 10 or 14 consecutive days**!

Resistance to antibiotics is increasingly common nowadays, and this is most true in the case of salmonellas. There are few antibiotics that are really effective against paratyphoid for the flock. **A susceptibility test is certainly advisable before treatment, because**:

- the chances of us finding the right agent **blind** are not high

- lengthy treatment of the whole flock is **expensive**; ineffective medicine represents money wasted

- lengthy treatment disturbs the flock, and we only see the **damaging side-effects** of ineffective medicine

- we **waste valuable time**, during which our flock further deteriorates rather than improves – often to an irreparable level

Nowadays our experience is that the most effective agents against salmonellas are **enrofloxacin**, **norfloxacin**, **amoxicillin**, and **amoxicillin + clavulanic acid**. While these antibiotics have an effect inside the intestinal canal, they are well absorbed from it, and so they reach the pathogen even if it is well spread outside the intestines in the body's other organs. **Sulfonamide derivatives** are effective against salmonellas, as are **ampicillin** and **apramycin**, especially as these have been used relatively little in recent years. **Furazolidone** is also enjoying a revival, for similar reasons.

In principle, **gentamycin**, **spectinomycin** and **colistin** are also effective, but these are not absorbed from the gut, and so, if administered orally, are not able to reach pathogens scattered inside the system. They are effective if injected, but only in the last resort (if no other substance works) should the whole flock be burdened with injections every day for 10-14 days. (However, drugs not absorbed from the gut are highly useful for **preventive** – also targeted! – **"cleansing" treatments**, because they represent the least burden to the system when administered orally, but reach the pathogen, as the carriage of salmonellas in the infected specimen tends to be limited to the intestinal system.)

Many professionals advise the immediate vaccination of the freshly infected flock during antibiotic treatment. This can be a good technique, but should only be implemented after careful consideration. Firstly, we should not use vaccines containing live pathogens, for these will be ruined by the antibiotics. To avoid this, we can administer vaccines that contain killed salmonellas, but if the birds are freshly infected, ill, or the disease is latent, the vaccination of the flock, alongside the extra burden, can itself prompt the illness to break out. In addition, we cannot expect vaccination to have great results with such a flock, as the unhealthy specimens will not have an adequate immune response to the vaccines administered to them. For all these reasons, the effectiveness of vaccination in such circumstances is often questionable.

Yet there are occasions when we have to vaccinate "in the heat of things", that is a flock suffering from an acute illness. On such occasions, the obviously ill specimens should be separated; only healthy animals should be vaccinated, so they are not. The others are all vaccinated, but we should be prepared for a strong negative reaction afterwards. A further risk is that the presence of unvaccinated specimens will prevent the immune level of the flock from being uniform for a long period.

There are those who try to avoid this danger by vaccinating all the pigeons, including the ill ones. This solution is even less wise. On the one hand, there will be a large number of deaths after vaccination; on the other hand, many of the pigeons that survive will not respond to the vaccine because of their weakened state. The result is a flock with differing immune states; from the point of view of eliminating salmonellosis, that is, we have achieved nothing. We would do better to observe the following schedule.

Method and general tasks to be performed when paratyphoid appears

- Separation of ill birds, extermination of severely ill specimens. Quarantining the flock. Taking samples for bacteriological and antibiotic susceptibility tests. Provision of vitamins, organic acids and immunostimulants in drinking water until the results arrive.

- Targeted antibiotic treatment of the entire flock, based on the lab results, over a period of at least 10 days. Individual treatment of severely ill birds. Depending on the type of antibiotic and the method of its application, the use of vitamins and immune boosters.

- Repeated lab tests before the end of treatment; the period of treatment may be extended in the light of the results.

- Adding probiotics to drinking water for 5 days to restore normal intestinal flora.

- After the illness has abated and the flock has recovered its strength, every single pigeon should be vaccinated simultaneously, accompanied by vitamins and immune boosters. It is best if we have a vaccine prepared against the particular strain of pathogen that is present, and only use this flock-specific vaccine.

- Two weeks after this vaccination, the separated, cured and vaccinated birds are allowed to rejoin the others.

- Thorough cleaning and disinfecting during the entire treatment period.

- The preventive vaccination should be repeated every six months.

The above are general guidelines. The methods of treatment should always be determined for the particular flock, and for each pathogen, depending on the given circumstances. Finding the most effective solution – based on the results of additional tests – is the job of the veterinarian, and ordering the course of treatment and continuous inspection of the flock both require veterinary cooperation.

Naturally, training must be suspended for the period of the treatment, and afterwards we must observe a further **two or three weeks of rest** before we start flying our pigeons again.

Prevention

As salmonellas are highly widespread, and remain virulent for a very prolonged period both inside and outside the body, it is very difficult to provide protection against them. It is absolutely essential that foreign specimens be put in quarantine before being entered into the flock. Again, we emphasize that seemingly healthy pigeons can also carry the pathogen and release it in great quantities – often this is precisely a type of salmonella that the residents of the loft have never encountered before.

Veterinary inspection of new specimens during quarantine is highly recommended, which should be accompanied by bacteriological testing of faeces (and other excretions). This tells us whether the pigeon releases salmonellas or not, and what antibiotics we should use if required.

Here we draw the reader's attention to a particular characteristic of paratyphoid: the pigeon carrying salmonella typically **releases the pathogen intermittently** rather than continuously. So, from the paratyphoid point of view, a negative lab result must always be taken with a pinch of salt, and if we are unsure it is better to repeat the test a number of times.

It is a fundamental rule that pigeons suffering from salmonella-related illness should not be taken to races, shows, markets, etc. Not only does this represent extremely unethical and unsportsmanlike behaviour – we must also bear in mind that an ill pigeon is more prone to picking up other pathogens, with which it can infect our own flock.

As salmonellas represent a large threat to young birds, and also to eggs, with endangered flocks we recommend a **preventive, cleansing 10-day treatment with antibiotics**, beginning **20 days before** mating. We must pay careful attention to two things. First, certain types of antibiotics have a detrimental effects on the fertility of eggs, and must not be used! Secondly, preventive treatment is only of real value if it takes place in a targeted fashion, that is, if it based on the results of bacteriological tests.

For this preventive treatment, it is advisable to administer antibiotics that are not absorbed from the gut. They do not put a burden on internal organs, but they do deplete or even eliminate pathogens hiding in the intestines. As they are not absorbed, they have no negative effect on reproduction or egg fertility.

Experience shows that amoxicillin does not have a negative effect on fertility, either, and so – although it is absorbed from the gut – it can also be administered around the breeding season.

If possible, we should **choose an antibiotic to which** the test shows that **normal intestinal bacteria are resistant**! Following antibiotic treatment, however, we should administer **probiotics for 4-5 days**, even in this instance.

*

Like coli, salmonellas do not like an **acidic environment**. We should strive to ensure that the **floor** of the loft and the **equipment** we use be acidic, and that drinking water be gently acidified with apple vinegar (slightly less than a tablespoon of 5% apple vinegar for one litre of drinking water) or a similar acidic product! The pigeons should be provided with probiotics on a regular basis, for it is by acidifying the **contents of the gut** that beneficial bacteria prevent pathogens from overgrowing in the intestinal system.

It is also in the interest of acquiring normal (beneficial) bacterial flora that young pigeons are sometimes **fed directly from the floor**. The desired intention of this is that the young quickly obtain normal intestinal bacteria via the droppings of the older pigeons. This technique can be useful, but **only if the flock is healthy and stable**, otherwise it is precisely the spread of pathogens (salmonella, coli) that we help with it. If we do use this method, we must take care that the floor be dry and cleaned on a regular basis, else the coccidia hiding in moist faeces over a number of days will become virulent and make the young ill.

Vaccination

To develop active protection against salmonellas, there are vaccines at our disposal which contain one or more types of salmonella. Depending on the vaccine, the pigeon must be at least 4-6 weeks old when the vaccination takes place, and birds that have already been vaccinated must receive a booster shot every six or twelve months. **Every member of the flock must be vaccinated at once, or soon after one another! If there are unvaccinated pigeons in the loft** – even older ones – birds of varying immune states infect one another, release of bacteria becomes continuous, as does the appearance of diseased birds. For all these reasons **the loft becomes incapable of regaining its epidemiological composure**, cannot reach the level required, and as a result **paratyphoid flares up continuously even without infection from outside**, which can only be subdued temporarily, with (expensive and systematic) antibiotic treatment.

The administering of antibiotics is not advised in the five days before and after a vaccination, as this can decrease the latter's effectiveness. (Exceptions to this are vaccinations comprising killed bacteria. As they do not contain live pathogens, the antibiotic cannot harm them.) We should take care that the flock we vaccinate be as healthy and with as high an immune state as possible, for this is how pigeons are weakened the least by the vaccination, and the highest level of protection will develop. To increase the chance of success, we should provide a mixture of vitamins and **immune boosters before, during and after the vaccination**. The protection induced will be stronger and longer-lasting as a result.

Unfortunately, what will be discussed in more detail concerning circovirus also holds true for salmonella vaccinations: circovirus infection greatly decreases the immune level of the flock, and therefore **strongly interferes with the effect of any vaccination**. It explains why outbreaks occur after even the most professionally performed vaccinations: the bird's immune system is simply unable to provide an adequate response to the vaccination. For this reason it is very important that **young birds be vaccinated as early as possible against paratyphoid, paramyxovirus and, if necessary, against pox**, before they run the risk of being infected with circovirus.

If we vaccinate pigeons grown for their meat against paratyphoid, we must be sure to take account of the withdrawal period before it can be culled for meat. We must not kill the bird or sell it as food before this period is over! Furthermore, there are vaccines that must not be used at all with pigeons bred for their meat!

Important!

There are many types of salmonella that are pathogenic to pigeons, while vaccines only contain one or a few types of (attenuated or killed) salmonella. There are similarities between the various types of salmonella, which is why a vaccine containing only a few types can also offer protection against the other types, though this protection is usually less strong. It can also happen that our flock becomes infected with an entirely new, exotic (foreign) type of salmonella, which is very different from the one in the vaccine, and thus the vaccination is even less effective. For all these reasons, it is possible that in a few weeks or a month paratyphoid illnesses will appear sporadically, even in a properly vaccinated flock with a high immune state.

Why is it so important to draw attention to this possibility? Because **it can make it seem as if the vaccination is unsuccessful**, thereby undermining our faith in the necessity and effectiveness of vaccines, possibly causing some fanciers to stop using them. This would be a grave mistake, however, because **even if an illness appears in a vaccinated flock, it causes immeasurably less damage** than if the flock is unvaccinated and therefore unprotected.

*

Public health implications

Like birds and other mammals, **human beings are also susceptible to salmonellas**. A salmonella infection is particularly dangerous, and can even be fatal, for children, the elderly, and those whose state of health is weak. Neither does getting over the illness necessarily mean that the pathogens are eliminated. Particularly if infected with a so-called exotic type, one brought from far away and unknown locally, a human can often become a carrier of salmonellas, remaining infectious for many years. Neither is it rare for repeated faecal tests to show negative results after overcoming the illness, then, all of a sudden – because the immune system has become weakened for other reasons – pathogens previously hiding in the system begin proliferating and releasing themselves again.

Although it is most often the Copenhagen variant that causes illness in pigeons, and this variant is generally less pathogenic to humans, it is still capable of bringing illness to those with decreased immunity. For this reason, it is very important to maintain a high level of personal hygiene: we should always wash our hands thoroughly after dealing with pigeons, and this is particularly vital before eating meals.

E. coli

Escherichia coli was one of the first single-cell organisms to be discovered. Coli bacteria can be harmless residents of the gut, but often they are capable of causing serious, possibly fatal illness in birds and mammals.

Transmission

The majority of E. coli strains reside permanently and usually harmlessly in the pigeon's intestinal system. In general, they live in equilibrium with the host's body, but if this equilibrium is upset for some reason, the coli bacterium can proliferate wildly, leading to (possibly serious) illness, even if the bird did not previously display any symptoms. That is to say, for an illness to develop it is not absolutely necessary for an infection to be passed from one pigeon to another. It is enough for there to be some kind of **weakening factor** within the digestive tract, such as a significant presence of coccidia. Another possibility is that a **strongly pathogenic** coli strain infects the flock – on such occasions sporadic illness can develop even if no additional factors make the pigeons susceptible. The ill specimens then begin to release the infectious pathogens in such quantities that the immune systems of even highly-resistant pigeons are exhausted by the level of their intake, and the other birds also become ill.

The wide distribution of the pathogen means that encounter with the most common coli strains usually takes place in the first hours of the pigeon's life. Neither is it rare for eggs to become infected, which can even happen within the body of the hen.

Damage

The severity and frequency of illness decreases with age. The greatest danger is presented by massive infection **within the egg or when the chick is a few days old**, especially if the strain has a high capacity to cause illness. The egg dies, or the chick that emerges will not be fit to live, and will soon perish. In a **young pigeon**, bacteria primarily spread in the lungs and the air sacs, then, once they break into the bloodstream, cause **toxaemia**. This results in severe inflammation of the spleen and liver, as well as degradation of the blood vessel walls, and a high proportion of the pigeons die.

Toxaemia is not usually present in **older pigeons**; rather, **localized** lung and air sac inflammation develops, sometimes in a chronic form. Neither is it rare for arthritis to appear.

If coli bacteria are highly proliferated in the gut, the poisonous substances they produce inflict direct damage on the intestinal wall, causing some degree of **diarrhoea**. Overly-proliferated coli can also break through the damaged intestinal wall into the bloodstream and reach a variety of organs, where they can cause acute, semi-acute or chronic inflammation.

The development of the disease is assisted by overcrowding, by lofts and nests being dirty with droppings, by draughts, humidity, and by feed that lacks vitamins (especially vitamin A).

Symptoms

Characteristic of the form of coli which causes intestinal inflammation is the release of large amounts of watery but typically phlegmatous intestinal content, that is whitish more than greenish, and which has a distinctive odour. The ill bird has no appetite, is dispirited, but drinks a lot. Vomiting is common, and for all these reasons the pigeon soon "**goes light**".

Bacteria scattered around the body may attack the lungs, the liver, the peritoneum, the walls of the air sacs, the joints, the ovaries, or the testicles. In the liver, lungs and kidneys, they can cause distinctive alterations like small necrotic conglomerations or granulomas. A characteristic deposit is formed on the peritoneum and the surface of the liver that is reminiscent of soaked wrapping paper, though this pathological finding is less typical in pigeons than, for example, in chicken or other poultry. Symptoms develop depending on which organs are damaged, e.g. respiratory problems, liver insufficiency, etc.

Like salmonellas, coli can also attack the **joints**, making pigeons display exactly the same symptoms as in the case of paratyphoid (swollen wing and/or foot joints, limpness, one or both wings drooping).

Coli can damage the ovaries or the testicles. Testicular inflammation can lead to infertility in males, while infection of the ovaries can cause embryos to die ("black egg" syndrome).

Young pigeons display more severe symptoms than ones that are growing up or already adults. A higher proportion fall victim to the illness: one of the main reasons for this – alongside toxaemia, which they are more susceptible to – is their faster dehydration from vomiting and diarrhoea.

Illness caused by coli bacteria are often **accompanied by mycoplasma strains**, which result in the emergence of respiratory problems.

*

Illnesses caused by coli must be distinguished from:

- **Salmonellosis**: because of embryo death, the large-scale death of young birds, the inflammation of joints, and infertility

- **Intestinal worms**: because of emaciation, diarrhoea, and stunted development
- **Canker**: because of the fast death of the young
- **Adenovirus:** similarly because of the high and fast rate of death among the young

Treatment

In theory, the coli bacterium is responsive to a broad range of antibiotics. In recent years, however, this responsiveness seems **to have declined strongly, in fact to a worrying degree**. One of the main reasons for this is to be found in courses of antibiotic treatment that are improperly administered, usually because they are started blindly or finished too abruptly. For illnesses caused by coli bacteria we strongly urge antibiotic treatment based on lab tests, and the selected antibiotic should be administered in the right quantity and for a sufficient length of time.

The period of **antibiotic treatment** for coli bacteria must be longer than the minimum of three days; at least **a five-day continuous course is recommended**. Nowadays it is the following that prove to be the most effective of the antibiotics available: amoxicillin, enrofloxacin, norfloxacin, spectinomycin and gentamycin. As we do not use them often, sulfonamide derivatives like sulfamethoxazole are also effective, as are products based on furazolidone. Resistance to apramycin is also low.

Unfortunately, we often encounter resistance to ampicillin, the main reason for which is that it has been widely used in small quantities, mixed into feed as a preventive supplement for farm animals (and thereby to increase their yield).

Because of the significant loss of fluid, the treatment must be accompanied by **the continuous provision of electrolyte (salt) solution**, which we strengthen by adding **glucose**. After the course of antibiotics we should administer **probiotics**.

Prevention

The use of vaccines against coli has not become common in everyday pigeon-breeding, and maybe there is no dire need for it. By reducing factors that help coli proliferate (overcrowding, coccidia, intestinal worms), with adequate provision of vitamins, and with regular cleaning and disinfecting, the damage caused by the bacteria can dependably be prevented, or at least reduced to the minimum.

Like salmonella, the coli bacterium prefers a gently alkaline environment. For this reason, we should always ensure that the pigeons' direct surroundings, particularly the floor of the loft, the surface of fixtures and drinking water, **should not be alkaline**. Unfortunately, an alkaline environment is precisely what many traditional disinfectants – principally lime – leave behind them; while this is less favourable for many other pathogens, it is ideal for coli and salmonella, the bacteria which give us the most headaches. So, if we use alkaline substances (like bleach) for disinfection, we should always make the floor of the loft and the trays **lightly acidic** afterwards. The simplest method is to wash or sprinkle the floor with water containing vinegar, or treat the drinking water with apple vinegar. During and after washing or sprinkling with vinegar, we should take care not to enrich the air with acidic gases that affect respiratory passages.

Just as in the case of salmonellas, the systematic administering of probiotics can greatly contribute to the prevention of the damage caused by coli.

Mycoplasmas

Mycoplasmas are single-cell creatures that represent a half-way house between bacteria and viruses. They are smaller and simpler in structure than bacteria, and one of their important characteristics is that they do not have cell walls. From this it follows that any antibiotics that attack cell walls (e.g. penicillin derivatives) have no effect on mycoplasmas.

Mycoplasmas are not very resistant creatures. Even hiding in discharges released into the outside world, they can only survive for a day or two. Traditional disinfectants destroy them within minutes.

Transmission

Most forms of mycoplasmas are highly prevalent in the environment. They are present in small numbers in the bodies of most pigeons on a continuous basis, but, because they are in equilibrium with the immune system, do not produce any symptoms. They only attack **if the pigeon's resistance is weakened for some reason**, when they start to spread, causing serious, possibly fatal, illness.

Mycoplasmas principally reach the outside world inside discharge from the ill pigeon, and infect through respiration or by mouth.

Damage

In the first instance they attack the eyes and the respiratory system, and so can be particularly damaging in racing pigeon flocks. The pathogen attacks the mucous membranes of the respiratory passages, causing inflammation of the mucosa of the throat and nose, and conjunctivitis. Spreading further, it damages the lower respiratory passages, the lungs, the walls of the air sacs, and also the abdominal membrane (peritoneum).

A typical way in which mycoplasmas spread infection is through the egg. If the egg is also infected with other pathogens (salmonella, coli), the embryo will probably die, or a chick will hatch that will not survive. If the egg is only infected with mycoplasma, the chick hatches, but is infected from day one.

As mycoplasmas are present in the pigeon's body on an almost continuous basis, there is no need for it to be infected from outside for illness to break out. **Any circumstance that weakens the pigeon's immune system** can cause the existing balance between the mycoplasma and the body to be upset: the mycoplasmas are freed from the restraints imposed by the host system, and proliferate wildly, generating the illness that is characteristic of them. Such a circumstance is often the primary attack of some other pathogen (which can be a virus, bacterium or even parasite), sustained stress, or, **most likely of all, overcrowding**. The insufficiency of air hygiene caused by the latter (bad quality air, or too strong ventilation used to counter it) **necessarily** causes mycoplasmas to flare up.

Symptoms

The first symptoms can include damage to the upper respiratory passages, the conjunctivae going red, lachrymation, and watery nasal discharge. If we hold a bird in the first stage of the illness close to our ear, we will hear a very quiet but distinctive chugging sound when each breath is taken. The birds' eagerness and capacity to fly are reduced. The tissue of the respiratory passages, damaged by the mycoplasma, can suffer secondary (if not tertiary) attack from other pathogens, which leads to a widening and worsening of symptoms, and, in the absence of treatment, even death.

Treatment

The **complete eradication of mycoplasmas from a specimen is difficult**, and is at best temporary, as it quickly becomes infected all over again. **It is also unnecessary**. The system of a pigeon whose general condition and immune state is good defeats the pathogen of its own accord, or at least keeps it under continuous inspection. We only need to treat against mycoplasma if these supposed pathogens proliferate too wildly in a system weakened in some way (stress, primary disease).

Antibiotics that are ineffective against them include penicillin derivatives like amoxicillin, ampicillin and cephalosporin. Typically, the most effective agents are the following: **enrofloxacin**, **norfloxacin**, **erythromycin**, **lincomycin**, **tylosin**, **tiamulin**, **sulfachlorpyridazine**, **chlortetracycline** and **oxytetracycline**, and, last but not least, **doxycycline**.

The period of treatment with antibiotics should be 4-5 days, but this is only sufficient if **the factor making the bird disposed to mycoplasmosis is eliminated** within this time. If it is not, the illness will re-emerge soon after the medication is stopped.

The antibiotic treatment should be accompanied with immune boosters and vitamin mixtures. After the course of treatment we should give the flock probiotics for a few days.

Note

As the pathogen only attacks if there is already some problem with the conditions in which the birds are kept (that is, with prevention of epidemics, hygiene, or excessive burdens), we can also consider the appearance of mycoplasma symptoms as **a kind**

of warning sign. If mycoplasma has flared up, we must of course treat against it, but in addition we must also research into and eliminate the **original causes** that have precipitated it.

As we mentioned above, experience shows that one of the most common reasons for the development of mycoplasmosis is overcrowding within the loft. It does no harm to observe the old saying: every pigeon needs a perch, but not every perch needs a pigeon.

Ornithosis
(Chlamydiosis)

Chlamydias, which cause ornithosis, **represent a half-way house between bacteria and viruses**. Certain antibiotics have an effect on them, and in this sense they are similar to bacteria. But, like viruses, they are parasites within the cells of the body under attack, destroying them from within. Culturing them requires specific conditions – they will not proliferate using ordinary culturing methods.

Transmission

Chlamydias are **highly virulent**, and can make a number of bird and mammal species ill. They can also cause serious, even fatal diseases in humans.

The pathogen principally spreads through respiratory discharge and via coughs and sneezes, but it can also reach the outside world in infectious form in the faeces or crop milk of the ill bird.

Most often, chlamydias attack the **eyes** and the tissue of the respiratory system, but in a weakened specimen they are capable of damaging any organ, causing serious, possibly fatal disease. Young birds respond much more sensitively, and become more seriously ill than adults do: in a flock that is neglected, the rate of death among the young can be as high as 70-80%! Older birds can display the more critical forms of the disease if under prolonged and significant stress.

Important!

Seemingly healthy adult birds can be symptom-free carriers of chlamydia, thus posing a risk both to the other pigeons and to the fancier!

Symptoms

The first symptom, when alterations to organs are not yet visible, is when pigeons begin to **rub and scratch the area of the eye** – usually just one – and the area on the side of the head. The affected conjunctiva soon goes red, and lachrymation can be seen, first clear, then purulent, which can be accompanied by a runny nose. Later, respiratory symptoms also emerge. The latter are not noticeable to begin with, possibly only appearing and worsening during and after flight. As the illness progresses, the pathogen attacks ever deeper tissues, reaching the lungs and the air sacs, when distinct respiratory difficulties and a rattling, sighing sound appear.

At a secondary level, pyogenic bacteria can also accompany the inflammation of the conjunctiva. In the absence of treatment, these can cause inflammation of the whole of the eye, which can lead to total destruction of the organ and thereby to **complete blindness**.

The illness is accompanied by lack of appetite and **typically deep green, glutinous diarrhoea**. The weight of the ill bird declines, it becomes thin, and sooner or later it dies.

In addition to bacteria, chlamydial illness is sometimes aggravated by an **associated fungal infection** (Aspergillus fumigatus) – necrotic and inflamed plexa develop, primarily on the walls of the air sacs and on the surface of the lungs.

When performing an autopsy, we usually find serious inflammation of the lungs, air sacs, peritoneum and pericardium. The spleen is very distended, typically taking on a protracted shape.

Illnesses caused by chlamydias **must be distinguished** from diseases with similar symptoms, particularly from **mycoplasma outbreaks**, which are relatively common. However, such a differential diagnosis cannot be established by routine examination alone. Demonstrating the existence of chlamydial infection with certainty is no easy task, not even with the use of additional tests. For if a blood test is conducted, this only tells us whether the pigeon has encountered the pathogen, but offers no information about its current state (whether it is still infected or free of it).

The presence of the pathogen can be proved directly by taking a swipe from the cornea. Fresh droppings can also be examined with a rapid test, but this technique is still not common in many countries, even though this issue is so significant for public health.

Under laboratory conditions, the pathogen can be identified in the liver or spleen of a dead bird, thus demonstrating chlamydial infection for certain.

Treatment

If we suspect the presence of chlamydial illness, we should inform a veterinarian without fail, as the disease is dangerous for animal and public health alike! If chlamydia appears, the whole flock must be treated, irrespective of how many pigeons have fallen ill, or whether they are still alive or not.

The flock must be **treated over a prolonged period**: the length of the therapy, including follow-up treatment, can be as long as thirty days (or more)! As culturing chlamydia is not a routine procedure, however, the treatment is not usually targeted. And yet, precisely because of the long period of treatment, it may be advisable to grow a simple culture from the droppings, for this will show whether there are any possible antibiotics which do not have an effect on the normal bacteria currently present in the gut.

Penicillin derivatives (amoxicillin, ampicillin) have absolutely no effect on the pathogens. The most expedient form of treatment is to use some **tetracycline derivative, combined with tylosin if necessary**.

In the course of the prolonged therapy, it is common for all or most of the **normal intestinal bacteria** to be destroyed. At the same time, **the role of these bacteria in helping digestion and producing vitamins is lost**, which, due to the long duration of the treatment, can be highly detrimental to the system. To help this, we can first ensure that B and K vitamins are administered continuously throughout the lengthy treatment, in order to compensate for the vitamins that would be produced by intestinal bacteria. Secondly, we should, if at all possible, choose the antibiotic that is least harmful to the useful residents of the gut (see above). In general, we can say that of the tetracyclines it is doxycycline that is least harmful to these good bacteria as it passes through the body. It also has the advantage that, compared to chlortetracycline and oxytetracycline, it is less toxic for the system, which for a course lasting many weeks is a significant consideration. It is also important constantly to add vinegar to drinking water: on the one hand, this helps the absorption of tetracyclines, and on the other hand it goes some way to make up for the acidic effect of the metabolic by-products of intestinal bacteria.

When chlamydial illness appears, and for many months afterwards, we must **disinfect more stringently and regularly** than usual.

Note

If ornithosis is worsened by a secondary fungal infection, treatment of the ill birds is a hopeless task, as the prolonged dosage of antibiotics only helps the fungal infection to spread further, and its symptoms become intensified. In cases of secondary fungal infection, or if we have reason to suspect it (a pigeon does not respond to antibiotics, or its symptoms only worsen) the specimens suspected of being infected must be destroyed as soon as possible, because there is no hope for their recovery, and their weakened systems release the pathogens in enormous numbers.

Prevention

As the pathogen is widespread, we can only defend against it with consistent procedures to prevent epidemics and by keeping the loft clean at all times. Bearing in mind that it can be carried without any symptoms being displayed, we should never allow a new pigeon into the flock without being **quarantined**.

At present, there are many countries in which there is no pigeon vaccine available for ornithosis.

Public health

Chlamydia can be passed on to humans. It generally causes a prolonged influenza-like illness that does not want to go away, but in the case of sensitive individuals (children, the elderly, or those suffering from other illnesses), its consequences can even be fatal. If we have any reason to suspect chlamydia, we should consult a doctor immediately!

Haemophilus

In pigeons, the bacterium Haemophilus paragallinarum causes an illness that **breaks out suddenly and spreads quickly**, and which is typically **limited to the upper respiratory passages**.

Pathogen

Haemophili are sensitive bacteria that are hard to grow in artificial conditions. It is only within the body that they are capable of surviving for a longer period; in the outside world they die within a day or two. Traditional disinfectants are effective against them.

Transmission

The illness spreads quickly within the loft, and a large proportion of the pigeons fall ill within a few days. The pathogen primarily infects via coughs and sneezes, or through drinking water and feed.

It is common for the infection to be brought in from outside (by new birds). Older specimens can **carry the pathogen without displaying any symptoms**, only to release it in great quantities in response to stress.

Symptoms

Under normal conditions, the main characteristic of the illness is that the proliferation of the bacterium, and thus of the symptoms, is limited to the head and the upper respiratory passages. The illness begins with copious serous nasal discharge, soon followed by severe conjunctivitis, which typically affects both eyes. The eyelids become very obviously swollen, and a viscous-purulent discharge is released from them, which can stick them together completely. In addition to a decline in consumption of feed, **the level of water drunk also decreases significantly**.

It is principally in flocks kept in unfavourable conditions that other bacteria like mycoplasmas accompany the illness in a secondary fashion. On such occasions the lower respiratory passages, the lungs and the air sacs can also become inflamed.

Treatment

The whole of the flock has to be treated. As it is hard to grow cultures of the bacteria, the antibiotic is usually selected without resort to a susceptibility test. The following agents are effective in theory and often used in practice: **enrofloxacin**, **norfloxacin**, **amoxicillin**, **tetracyclines**, **sulfachlorpyridazine combined with trimethoprim**, and **erythromycin**.

We should be sure to administer a product containing vitamin A alongside the antibiotics. The treatment should last for at least five days, after which we should give probiotics over a period of 4-5 days.

Should mycoplasmosis appear as a secondary illness, the antibiotics mentioned above are effective against it as well, and so it is not generally necessary to provide separate treatment with other antibiotics. An exception to this is amoxicillin, which has no effect on mycoplasmas. If there is any suspicion that mycoplasmosis is present (if lower respiratory symptoms appear, for example), then we should use an agent other than amoxicillin!

2. Virus-induced diseases

About viruses in general

Viruses are pathogens that are smaller than bacteria, and which cannot be seen under an ordinary microscope. To observe them directly, we need the hundreds of thousands times magnification power of an electron microscope.

Unlike bacteria, viruses are not capable of independent life, and neither can they proliferate on their own. They do not have their own metabolism. It follows that **antibiotics will have no effect on them**. For their proliferation, or more precisely their multiplication, they use the cells of the body they attack, forcing the cell to stop its usual activities and build the constitutive elements of the virus in enormous numbers. After multiplying in this way, and once freed from the cell that is condemned to destruction, they go on to attack newer and newer cells and tissues.

Viruses tend to be specific to a species, that is a given strain of a virus is only capable of bringing illness to creatures of particular species. Pigeon pox virus cannot infect geese, for example, just as goose influenza virus is incapable of harming pigeons.

However, viruses are capable of changing fast, that is of mutation, which **fundamentally** transforms their existing characteristics. Such large mutations, or rather their manifestation, are relatively rare, but their consequences can be extraordinary. Paramyxovirus in pigeons, which was unknown before the 1980s, is also the result of such a mutation. The Newcastle disease virus (avian pneumoencephalitis virus which is also paramyxovirus), of which we have long been aware, underwent such a mutation that it gave birth to paramyxovirus in pigeons, which has quite different properties.

As a result of mutation, the genetic composition of the virus changes to some degree, and so the virus strain that spreads from it is given new properties. Maybe it will infect a different species of animal, or maybe it will "stay" with the old one, but display a much stronger capacity to infect, or, for example, it may attack other organs or tissues within the body. Equally, the virus can be "tamed" by such a change, and only cause illnesses with a milder effect than before. It is this circumstance that we take advantage of when we vaccinate pigeons with pathogenic viruses that have (artificially) been attenuated in this way.

Unlike bacteria, culturing of viruses requires sophisticated equipment and special conditions, just as does the detection of their presence in a given organ. However, it is relatively quick and easy to detect the presence of virus-specific **antibodies** produced by the immune system when it encounters the virus. We must take two things into account when evaluating a positive result of this kind, however. Firstly, the detection of an antibody only tells us that the body has encountered the virus at some stage, and is no proof that the virus is still present in the system at the time of the test. Secondly, the test gives a positive result even if the pigeon has never met the wild "street" incarnation of the virus, but has at some point been vaccinated against such a virus, i.e. been administered with an attenuated or killed virus.

*

From the point of view of veterinary treatment, one of the most important distinctions between bacterial and viral illnesses is that antibiotics (in theory) have an effect on bacteria, but not on viruses. That is, viral diseases cannot directly be influenced with antibiotics, and so it is up to the body's immune system to deal with the viruses attacking it. There are nevertheless **certain viral illnesses** for which treatment with antibiotics is advisable, but we use this not to control the virus, but rather **the bacteria making a secondary attack following the viral infection**.

It follows from the above that viral illnesses are capable of causing severe damage to pigeons, and so **we must place particular emphasis on their prevention**. We must strive to eliminate or confine them with regular vaccinations, the strict observance of rules to prevent epidemics, and by ensuring optimal hygienic conditions.

* * *

In the following sections we present the most important illnesses in pigeons that are caused by viruses. We briefly characterize the various pathogens, their methods of transmission and infection, the damage they cause to the system, and how to defend pigeons against them.

Paramyxovirus

The disease caused by paramyxovirus in pigeons typically has a clinical picture with neurological symptoms and that is highly contagious. Since its first appearance, it quickly spread over most of the world, **causing immense damage** to pigeon flocks in infected areas.

History

The virus causing the illness probably came into being in North Africa at the start of the 1980s, from where it spread to Italy, then infected other Mediterranean countries and soon the whole of the Continent. This was followed by Great Britain, then North America.

The variant of paramyxovirus causing illness in pigeons (pigeon PMV for short) developed from a mutation of the Newcastle disease virus, a paramyxovirus that does not affect pigeons. The mutant virus was already capable of attaching itself to certain cells in the pigeon's body, penetrating them, proliferating, and inducing the disease and the severe symptoms it brought with it. As pigeons had never encountered this new pigeon PMV before, its attack took their immune systems almost completely by surprise. Only almost, because some had already experienced the original paramyxovirus (the virus causing Newcastle disease in chickens). While this virus does not cause illness in pigeons, thanks to the strong structural similarity, it provides a certain level of cross-protection against pigeon PMV. Albeit to a lesser degree, the similar structure literally acts as a reminder to the body's immune system should the pigeon be attacked by pigeon PMV. It is this cross-protection that we make use of when immunizing birds against pigeon PMV by use of the Newcastle disease virus.

Note

Paramyxoviruses include the viruses that cause measles in humans and distemper in dogs. These virus strains are highly species-specific, that is they are only capable of infecting one or a very few species. At any one given point in time, at least. Pigeon PMV is an example of how completely new strains of a virus can develop unsuspectedly and unpredictably, and how they attack one particular species. We could also take the example of the parvovirus responsible for diarrhoea in dogs, the result of a mutation of a virus causing illness in cats, which spread all over the world and within a short space of time destroyed almost a third of dogs susceptible to it.

Transmission

Pigeon PMV is a **highly contagious pathogen**, i.e. one that spreads easily from one flock to the next, and which in a responsive (unvaccinated) flock can infect a large number of specimens. In a high proportion of cases of infection, **especially in the young, it can cause death**. Inside the body, the virus breaks into the bloodstream, reaches most organs, as a result of which it can, in theory, be released in any discharge from the infected pigeon's body. It infects susceptible pigeons via their eyes, nose and mouth.

Despite this, pigeon PMV typically **spreads relatively slowly** from pigeon to pigeon within the infected loft. Formerly, when preventive vaccination was not yet common practice, this provided an opportunity for fanciers quickly to vaccinate an infected flock to stop the virus from spreading to uninfected birds, and thus to save the majority of their pigeons. The days of this are largely gone, however, as the virus has since become so widespread that **preventive protection** against it is a common if not obligatory part of pigeon-breeding the world over.

The characteristic of illnesses causes by pigeon PMV is their **long incubation period**. The time from infection to the appearance of the first symptoms is rarely as short as a week, and more often many weeks, maybe six, but incubation periods as long as twelve weeks have also been known! In an unvaccinated, susceptible flock, this fact makes prevention of an epidemic difficult if not impossible, as it would extend the length of quarantine to three months, which is not a realistic requirement in practice. This is another reason, then, for the regular vaccination of the flock.

The damage inflicted by the virus can most often be seen in flocks of racing pigeons where the young birds were not vaccinated in time. The older pigeons bring home the virus when they return from races, and although they do not get ill themselves (assuming they have received the vaccination in time themselves, of course!), they infect the defenceless young age-group, thereby causing a large number of deaths amongst it.

Damage

After entering a susceptible body, pigeon PMV starts by attacking the cells near the point of infection. It multiplies inside them, then after the cells are destroyed it breaks into the bloodstream, and is thus capable of reaching just about any cell in the body. Yet its greatest affinity (we could almost say attraction) is to the cells of the **central nervous system**, or those of the **kidneys**.

Upon entering a susceptible animal, the virus infects irrespective of age. So in the case of pigeon PMV there is no immunity that develops as birds get older, as in the case of circovirus, for example. Thus it is primarily with vaccinations that we can hope to provide protection against it, i.e. with active immunization, though specimens that survive the illness will also develop immunity.

Symptoms

As the virus principally attacks the nervous system and the kidneys, and to a lesser extent the cells of the intestinal wall, its major symptoms also involve these organs.

Neurological symptoms are the most common. The pigeons' heads tremble, they twist their necks in a funny way, sometimes so much that the top of their heads points to the ground. Their movements are disordered, they often spin around, stagger and lurch about, and do backwards cartwheels. Those with such severe symptoms cannot possibly consume their feed, but consumption of water and food can be a problem even for those with milder symptoms. The illness can also be accompanied by lameness, with one or both of the pigeon's wings drooping, and there can also be weakness in the legs.

The other typical symptom is large amounts of **watery "diarrhoea"**, sometimes released almost continuously, which makes the floor of the cage look as if it had been hosed down. We put the term diarrhoea in inverted commas because the discharge is not from the gut, and therefore **does not represent real diarrhoea**. The large amount of liquid is released from the kidneys under attack by the virus: the damaged kidney tissues are not capable of performing their function of making urine concentrated, and so it becomes abnormally watery and plentiful. If the intestinal wall are not yet damaged, we can see the excreted substance characteristic of the disease mixed in the cloaca on the floor of the loft: **a watery puddle, with a handful of stick-shaped, normal pieces of faeces in the middle**. This large-scale loss of water is accompanied by increased thirst, visible from frequent drinking of water – to the extent that the pigeons are still capable of consuming any. If not, they quickly become dehydrated and perish.

Experience suggests that both groups of symptoms are present in most cases, though there have been reports of instances where **one symptom was missing**; either neurological symptoms appeared, without abnormal urine excretion, or watery pseudo-diarrhoea was present, but with no damage to the nervous system. We note that greenish faeces were also reported in some cases, indicating secondary intestinal infection.

Sometimes a few of the infected young pigeons die suddenly without previously displaying any symptoms. In less acute instances the aforementioned symptoms can appear. Should illness be prolonged, young birds that survive for longer **fail to develop properly**. They may also show the watery **pseudo-diarrhoea**, and often suffer **disorders in growing plumage**.

Some older pigeons live through the disease while hardly displaying any symptoms at all. Their food consumption does not decrease, their behaviour is unchanged, but if taken to races **they are not able to perform at their best**. It is also observable that these birds, even though they hardly display the symptoms of pigeon PMV (if at all), are **much more likely to succumb to another infectious disease**.

Although pigeon PMV usually causes characteristic symptoms, the damage it causes can nevertheless sometimes be confused with other illnesses. For this reason, the disease caused by paramyxovirus in pigeons **must be distinguished from**:

- **paratyphoid**, because of its neurological symptoms
- **adenovirus type I**, because it can cause watery diarrhoea
- **adenovirus type II**, because it can make pigeons die suddenly
- **poisonings**, because of its neurological symptoms, and because it can cause lameness and sudden death

Treatment

Fanciers are often quick to get rid of birds that show the symptoms of pigeon PMV, saying that their recovery is hopeless in any case, and that they will only infect the others. While the latter claim is very true, the former is not correct. The vast majority of adult birds survive this illness, and in most cases **their recovery is total**: neither their race performance nor their reproductiveness is affected detrimentally. Tests conducted in a number of countries show that specimens who have been through the illness **do not become carriers of the virus**; in the light of all this, we should think hard whether to put pigeons down – particularly valuable ones that are not easy to replace – or whether we should make an attempt to save them.

Of course, helping pigeons with serious neurological symptoms to pull through the illness is lengthy and tiring work. But if we embark on this course, **we should first quarantine them** from the rest of the flock, then make preparations for treatment lasting one or two months, maybe even three(!). The survival of these pigeons depends more than anything else on whether they receive the required daily amount of drinking water and feed, which left to their own devices they are not usually able to consume. It is advisable to use moist feed, in small quantities at a time, but if possible a number of times each day. The feed must be placed directly in the throat. The feed must be **easy to digest** – we should avoid using beans or peas. We should provide drinking water from a suitable syringe, at least three times a day. Bearing in mind their bodies' sustained and substantial dehydration, which also represents a significant loss of salt and vitamins, we must pay careful attention to the supply of vitamin

B and electrolyte to the ill birds. Particularly effective is the regular provision of **vitamin C**, of **B vitamins enriched with mineral salts**, and of **glucose**. We must also **protect against secondary attacks** on the weakened body from other pathogens, if possible in a targeted way, on the basis of a secondary diagnosis.

In addition to the treatment of ill birds in quarantine, we must introduce some precautions for the **other, seemingly healthy pigeons**. Until the whole flock has pulled through the illness, or has been protected with **vaccinations that are performed as early as possible**, the pigeons should not be flown, and it is also advisable to postpone pairing. It is of course forbidden to take birds from the infected flock to markets, races, exhibitions, etc.

Emphasis must be placed on **daily cleaning** and disinfection, both in the quarantined area and in the other lofts. Droppings must be removed at least once a day, and disinfection should also take place as often as possible. We should only use disinfectants that are sure to be effective against viruses.

Note

When we decide whether to destroy pigeons made ill by PMV, or to try to help them to pull through it, we should take another consideration into account. As we saw, a small proportion of birds survive infection with the virus even if left to their own devices. If we give the birds our complete attention when treating them, the number of specimens that survive will increase. The point is that when the illness strikes there will be deaths, but there will also be survivors. It goes without saying that those pigeons will **survive** that have **stronger constitutions and immune systems** than their less fortunate friends. To a large extent, these characteristics are inherited, and so, if we give them a chance (i.e. if we do not put them down), they will pass on these valuable qualities to their descendants. We could also say that if we leave the illness to select the most viable pigeons, which then preserve this viability for future generations, **their descendants will most likely be more resistant** not only to paramyxovirus, but also to other pathogens.

Like all breeders, the pigeon fancier is inclined to follow the given breeding objective (e.g. maximizing flying performance), and, when choosing which birds to breed, only pays attention to factors directly linked to this objective, and no others, like the strength of the immune system, for example. Bearing in mind that newer and newer pathogens are attacking, maybe it is time to smuggle such health considerations back into the task of selection for breeding, even if in the short term they slow a breeder's attempts to produce the best results. In other words, **selection of pigeons should also reflect their general medical fitness.**

Perhaps it is instructive to look at similar breeding errors that occur with other species. It is well known that illnesses causing malformation of hip-joints in dogs have become widespread in recent years across the world. There are a number of factors that make a dog prone to the disease, but its increasingly common appearance is no doubt also due to breeding work which bases the selection of pedigree stock on performance criteria, e.g. better tracking ability, or on a more robust external appearance, ignoring important biomedical considerations. It is no accident that malformation of hip-joints is most common in working dogs (German shepherds, rottweilers). Unfortunately, such breeding-induced genetic problems at a species or breed level usually remain concealed for a long period, accumulating invisibly, before suddenly coming to the surface when they reach a certain level within a breed or species. Once this happens, desperate efforts to eradicate them will only be successful if other breeding objectives are temporarily or partially put to one side.

Prevention

Because pigeon PMV is highly contagious, and the incubation period of the illness it causes is long, the success of traditional measures to prevent epidemics becomes rather uncertain. For this reason, **successful protection against the virus is effectively impossible without regular vaccinations**. In general, we can say that the minimum level of protection is an annual booster shot for older pigeons that have already been vaccinated, and vaccination of young pigeons at the earliest possible opportunity.

Young pigeons can be vaccinated **from the age of three weeks**. The vaccination must take place at least two (but preferably more) weeks before the racing season for the older birds begins, because this is the minimum amount of time required for a certain level of protection against the virus to develop in the vaccinated system. (And we can raise this level with booster shots!) For it is certain the pigeons returning from races will bring the wild version of the virus back into the flock, and it will show no mercy in infecting and making ill the susceptible younger birds.

If the vaccination of the young has not taken place by this time, then as more susceptible specimens they must be kept apart from older pigeons that come and go from the lofts. The young pigeons are only allowed to leave the yard themselves at the earliest two weeks after their vaccination.

It is advisable to administer the annual booster shot for older pigeons in late autumn or winter, after moulting, but a number of weeks before pairing. We should not vaccinate stock birds during laying or rearing periods!

The above recommendations for vaccinations are general guidelines. In extreme situations (e.g. health problems within the yard, risk of an epidemic in the surrounding area) it is the task of the veterinarian to weigh up the circumstances and decide on any necessary modifications to the treatment.

*

We will cover this in detail during our discussion of **circovirus**, but we make brief mention of it here: vaccination of the young against pigeon PMV and other pathogens (salmonellas, pigeon pox virus) must happen as early as possible, for if circovirus infects them and attacks their immune system early, before the vaccine's protection is effective, we cannot expect the vaccinations to be very successful.

Circovirus

This is a new and very significant problem that in many places has not yet been recognized, and which is likely to cause enormous problems in pigeon-fancying in both the shorter and longer term.

History

Illnesses caused by circovirus have long been known in chickens and species of parrot. It was first found in pigeons in Canada in 1986. It was diagnosed in Australia three years later, and then in certain states in the US.

In chickens the virus causes anaemia, while in species of parrot the primary symptoms are disorders in plumage and beak formation. In recent years, however, circovirus has been found in other species of birds, including pigeons. It is likely that infection of pigeons with circovirus is much more widespread than we usually estimate, **because circovirus, although the cause or catalyst for very severe diseases, does not itself produce specific symptoms, and so its presence most often goes unnoticed.**

Transmission

It is probable that the virus primarily spreads via faeces. Though it may be present in the nasal or throat discharge of the infected pigeon, its transmission via drinking water or the air is as yet unproven. Neither is it clear which species of wild bird are infected with the virus and to what degree and with what intensity they release it into the surroundings.

Circoviruses are generally highly resistant to heat and to various disinfectants, and disposing of them requires great care.

Damage

In pigeons, circoviruses attack and destroy the cells of the lymphatic organs (the spleen, the thymus, the Bursa of Fabricius), which make up part of the body's defence mechanism, and so **they resemble HIV, which leads to AIDS in humans**. Afterwards, the weakened immune system is no longer capable of fighting other pathogens, either, and so **a specimen infected with circovirus can in theory fall ill from any pathogen**; indeed, **even harmless microbes** can attack it.

The virus primarily presents a danger for **young birds that are less than one year old**. Over the age of one, pigeons become more resistant, because an age-related immunity develops within them. (The reason for this is that a group of lymphatic glands, e.g. the Bursa of Fabricius, in which the virus would be capable of multiplication, naturally die away with age.) It has also been suggested that older specimens in many flocks have already lived through circovirus infection, which for some reason was not recognized at the time, e.g. if illnesses were mild, or if the reason for death was not established. Older birds that have survived the infection have probably developed effective protection against it, and thus been spared should it have attacked a second time.

Symptoms

It is not easy to recognize infection with circovirus in pigeon flocks, as the symptoms can vary along a highly broad spectrum, essentially depending on what other pathogens are accompanying the infection. These pathogens making a secondary attack can be bacteria, viruses, parasites, fungi, or a combination of these. So we should begin to suspect damage from circovirus if **a number of illnesses** rear their ugly head in the loft **within a short space of time**, and this is particularly suspicious if restricted to young birds.

In acute, severe cases, birds lose their appetite and become lethargic, and die within a few days. In less acute instances, the lethargy is accompanied by diarrhoea and loss in body weight, birds become incapable of flying, and only then do they die. Another common symptom is the presence of respiratory difficulties, accompanied by nasal discharge. In prolonged cases, birds slowly but surely become thinner. All these symptoms can be accompanied by diarrhoea, the nature of which is also variable: it is often mucous-gelatinous and greeny-brown, but it can be watery, too. In addition to this, secondary or tertiary infections can mean that **in theory symptoms characteristic of any other illness can also appear**.

Precisely because of the many types of possible symptoms, we can only determine circovirus infection for certain by the use of additional tests. This can take place in a direct fashion with the help of histological tests of the spleen, the Bursa of Fabricius, and other lymphatic organs. These are rarely carried out in the case of pigeons, however, which is one of the reasons why circovirus infection or illness is often not diagnosed. The more widespread use of simpler tests, which show whether the virus is or has been present, will be of great assistance in determining the prevalence of the virus.

Treatment

As viruses are not affected by antibiotics, we cannot fight the pathogen directly. The most important thing is ensuring optimal provisions for the pigeons, generally improving their strength, administering adequate vitamins, and **supporting the immune system in every way possible**. In addition, we must treat illnesses caused by the inevitable secondary infections with the relevant medicines, and do so as quickly and as precisely as possible. By precision we mean administering the correct dose of medicine in a targeted way, as we must do all we can to protect an already unstable system from an antibiotic that is often chosen arbitrarily (and thus ineffective), and/or given in too high a dose.

Dimethylglycine is an agent that deserves special mention as a drug that has recently become popular and enjoyed widespread praise. It is a compound that interacts with the bird's metabolism at many points. Its effectiveness has also been observed in connection to the treatment of other infectious diseases, and is particularly evident in the case of circovirus. Used as instructed, it has helped in countless seemingly hopeless instances. Dimethylglycine is particularly useful in treating circovirus illnesses, as there is only a narrow range of medicines that are genuinely effective.

We can also hope for assistance from products containing vitamins and trace elements, and from active ingredients that give direct support to the immune system. Thus, for example, immunoglobulins, "guest" antibodies imported into the pigeon's body, can have a good effect. (See chapter IV for further details.)

Prevention

At the present time **there is as yet no specific vaccine** for circovirus, and so we have to wait before we can provide active protection for our pigeons. It is probable that an effective vaccine will be available sooner or later – as happened in the case of paramyxovirus – but it is hard even to guess when this will be. If we look at the success of research into a vaccine for the similar HIV virus, we have no great cause for optimism. (Though it always possible that it is exactly the experiences of the fight against circovirus in pigeons that will assist a breakthrough in the struggle against HIV.)

Unfortunately, the very nature of pigeon racing makes it inevitable that our pigeons will meet infected specimens, and catch circovirus from them. Until a vaccine is brought into circulation, the only thing we can do is **to implement rules of prevention of epidemics as fully as possible** to prevent or at least delay infection of our flock, **paying particular attention to birds that are less than one year old**.

IMPORTANT!

In many countries there is still no real data on the incidence of circovirus in pigeon flocks. It is conceivable that a comprehensive survey would yield results as surprising as those found in Scotland. The virus was first identified there in 1994, and a recent research programme investigated the birds of 17 flocks. The results were devastating: in 14 cases out of 17, yards proved to be infected with circovirus.

The general picture is **just possibly** not quite this tragic, but we should certainly assume that infection with circovirus has a very negative effect. As it is the immune system that the virus damages, an affected specimen, **even if it does not appear ill, will react badly to the usual vaccinations, if at all**. For this reason, if for example we were to vaccinate a pigeon infected with circovirus against paramyxovirus, the vaccination will not be successful: no protection will develop against the paramyxovirus, as **the damaged immune system is incapable of providing a regular immune response to the paramyxovirus vaccine**. This is true for other vaccinations, too, and this is why fanciers (and sometimes veterinarians) are often confused when **a flock that has been vaccinated appropriately and repeatedly nevertheless becomes ill** with e.g. paratyphoid.

The situation is a serious one. In any case, this is further proof that we cannot successfully protect the health of our pigeon flocks with medicines and vaccines alone. In connection to circovirus infections, too, we can say that **traditional methods of protection seem to be regaining their value**: prevention of epidemics, a consistent high level of hygiene, keeping birds in a stress-free environment with comprehensive nourishment, which all guarantee that the immune system will remain at a high level. We should by all means ensure **strict measures of prevention of**

epidemics so that we protect young birds from becoming infected at least until they have received the most important vaccinations (more precisely, until those have taken their effect), as after any possible circovirus infection it is no use our vaccinating them against other illnesses. This is why **the vaccination against paramyxovirus must be performed as early as possible, when the pigeons are three weeks old!** In theory, we can vaccinate against paratyphoid from the age of four weeks, but this of course depends on a number of factors, including the vaccine used and when the vaccination against paramyxovirus takes place.

Adenoviruses

Two types of adenovirus cause illness in pigeons, and these are traditionally referred to as type I and type II.

History

Adenovirus type I was discovered in 1976. Type II was first identified in Belgium in 1992, and described as the pathogen of a disease causing sudden death in pigeons.

Pathogen

The resistance of adenoviruses is not high – traditional disinfectants destroy them within minutes. In secretions that are released into the environment (and not cleaned away!), however, they can remain infectious for weeks.

Transmission

Adenovirus **type I** causes illness in **young pigeons**, typically in the first six months of their life. The epidemic usually has its peak in **June**. (Northern Hemisphere)

The **type II** virus can make pigeons **of any age** ill, and it does not display the same seasonality as type I.

Damage, symptoms

The **type I** viruses infecting the young primarily attack the cells of the intestinal wall, causing **watery diarrhoea**. (This is genuine diarrhoea, as it comes from the gut, unlike the extensive release of liquid caused by paramyxovirus, which is from the kidneys!) The **coli** bacterium often makes a secondary attack on the weakened mucous membrane, making the diarrhoea even worse, and changing its consistence. The symptoms may be accompanied by **frequent vomiting**. **The crop is typically stuffed with feed**. Prolonged cases lead to weight loss.

Adenovirus **type II** primarily attacks liver cells, with the intestinal system often remaining (at least apparently) healthy. In the **liver** the virus **causes severe and extensive damage** which can **quickly** – within a day and a half or two days – **lead to death, whatever the pigeon's age**. The illness is otherwise typically symptom-free: if there is time for symptoms to develop, yellow diarrhoea and vomiting can occur before the bird dies. Autopsy reveals a liver that is yellowy, enlarged, and brighter than usual, speckled with necrotic areas that glisten a red colour.

The mortality rate is generally about 30%, but there have been cases where it has been 100% (!).

Because of the watery diarrhoea it causes, type I adenovirus must be distinguished from **paramyxovirus illnesses**; type II needs to be **distinguished from poisonings** because it damages the liver, produces vomiting, and/or causes sudden death.

Treatment

As we are talking about a virus, antibiotics have no direct effect either on type I or on type II. In the case of type I attacking the young, however, targeted antibiotic treatment is certainly justified: this therapy has an effect on **a secondary attack from coli bacteria**, and if we make a good choice of antibiotic, we can expect a good rate of survival.

Products containing immunoglobulins (IgG, IgA, IgM) can be very effective against type I of the illness, also referred to as young animals' disease. We note that these products also offer a certain level of protection against other infectious diseases. If administering them, however, we should be aware that vaccines given simultaneously or soon after one another can lessen each other's effectiveness! (For more details see chapter IV, section 2.)

In the case of the liver inflammation caused by type II, we can do no more than to try to save as many members of the flock as possible with **substances that protect the liver** and with vitamins. The outcome of the illness, that is the proportion of birds that fall victim to it, is highly dependent on the average immune state of the flock at the time of infection, and the conditions in which it is kept (overcrowding!).

Prevention

Our first defence against the virus is by observing rules of prevention of epidemics. If we experience a suspicious illness in the flock, we should try to identify or rule out the pathogen as quickly as possible, which requires a veterinary examination (including autopsy), but can also include additional laboratory tests.

Note

The frequency of damage caused by adenoviruses is not yet truly clear. It may be that they cause illness and death much more often than we think. Perhaps they are responsible for much damage that we put down e.g. to paramyxovirus. The illness caused by type I adenovirus can easily be confused with the form of the pigeon PMV infection where the pseudo-diarrhoea dominates over the neurological symptoms. A precise survey of the prevalence of adenovirus in pigeons is one of the tasks still ahead of us.

Pigeon pox

Like pox in other species of animal, pigeon pox is caused by a pathogen belonging to the big family of pox viruses. The disease has probably been widespread across the world since ancient times, and to this day is widely known among fanciers, and yet active protection against it – regular vaccination – is less commonly implemented.

Transmission

Amongst pigeons pox is typically **transmitted** by **blood-sucking arthropods**, especially, in warmer climates, by various types of mosquitoes. The peak periods for infections therefore coincide with the swarming times of mosquitoes and other blood-sucking arthropods. But, as the illness can be transmitted by lice, mites and ticks, it can also appear at other times.

In addition to being spread by arthropods, pox virus can be passed on via infected saliva in drinking water, via faeces, or **by direct contact**.

Spread of the virus is helped by its exceptionally high resistance, as – unlike the majority of viruses – once released from the body it can remain infectious for many years, even decades (!). This means that a new flock introduced into a yard can become infected, even if the yard was only infected a long time ago and has stood empty for years.

Note

Thanks to global warming, the number of arthropods in our environment increases every year, and indeed new types of insects are settling in areas with milder climates that previously only found the conditions necessary for survival in warmer climes. For this reason, we can also reasonably expect the prevalence of diseases transmitted by arthropods – like pox – to increase.

Damage

The virus attacks the epithelial cells **on the surface of the skin or the mucous membrane**. Even though it does not penetrate very deeply, it can nevertheless instigate serious changes, as it **opens a path** for other pathogens, like **pyogenic bacteria**, that are capable of sinking in further. Combined with the pox virus, these are capable of enough damage to lead to the bird's death. If the virus attacks the mucous membrane of the buccal cavity, in addition to milder local symptoms, the pain of consuming feed and thereby its insufficient intake leads to the bird becoming weaker and thinner.

Although all age-groups are susceptible to the virus, it is nevertheless **principally the young** that are sensitive to it. Nestlings that are one or two weeks old are still protected by immunity from the egg, while most members of the older age-group have acquired protection from having previously recovered from the disease. Despite this, a strong infection (large-scale virus) burdens the system even of adult birds enjoying immunity, and although it only rarely generates changes visible to the naked eye, it can cause flying performance to slacken.

The shortage of vitamin A that accompanies the infection can greatly exacerbate the symptoms that emerge.

Symptoms

In pigeons it is most often the **dry form** of pox that appears. Papilla-like growths and scabby deformations appear around the eyes, on the side of the beak, around the nostrils and on the legs. Wounds can also develop on skin covered with plumage.

In its **wet form**, pox starts by being as small as a grain of sand, then converging fibrous, greyish-yellow deposits appear within the buccal cavity, on the mucous membranes of the mouth and throat. In more severe variants of the wet form, swallowing and respiratory difficulties emerge, leading to weight loss, and in extreme instances to death.

Pathogens **making secondary attacks**, primarily pyogenic cocci, may settle on the epithelial wounds caused by the virus. Under normal conditions these are not capable of attacking healthy skin or mucous membranes, but the pox virus makes way for them to do so. **Pyogenic processes** develop on the skin, and/or inside the buccal cavity. These modifications can spread to the eyeballs, with a fibrous plug stopping the eye cavity, which can lead to atrophy of the eyeball.

The virus can occasionally break into the bloodstream, evoking fever, lethargy, and, within a few days, death.

The damage caused by the pox virus is often accompanied by **mycoplasmas**, and its symptoms and pathological picture are altered accordingly.

The incubation period of pigeon pox varies from 4 to 14 days; this is how long after the infection the first visible skin changes take place, which usually stay for many weeks. Alterations to the mucous membrane of the buccal cavity remain for even longer, maybe for months. Often, even before the characteristic skin changes develop, attention is drawn to the lurking illness by a **drastic decline in flying performance**.

The form of pigeon pox which spreads to the mucous membrane of the buccal cavity must be distinguished from deformations to the buccal cavity caused by trichomonads, and from fungal infections.

Treatment

If we observe skin symptoms, the correct procedure is to brush the affected areas twice a day with **iodic solution**, even if we know that the treatment will not make the skin deformations heal much more quickly. It is certainly useful, however, as on the one hand it prevents more serious, secondary purulent processes from developing, and on the other hand the pigeon will release far fewer infectious viruses into the surroundings. If we start the treatment late, and already see processes that are becoming purulent, we should, in addition to the iodic treatment, also make localized use of a cream containing antibiotics. If the purulence is serious and extensive, there may be a need for systemic antibiotic treatment, but this is rare.

We should follow a similar approach in the event of alterations to the mucous membrane, with the difference that the iodic solution must be diluted to five or ten times its volume.

We should not forget supplementary **immune boosters** and vitamins. Here it is particularly important to introduce sufficient **vitamin A** into the body to protect the epithelium. We should take care with dosage, as it is a member of the fat-soluble vitamin group that, if overdosed, easily accumulates in the system to such an extent that the effect is opposite to the one desired: excessive keratosis of the epithelial tissue, and thus only exacerbation of the process!

Prevention

As the virus is highly resistant, and arthropods have a role in its transmission, it is important that the loft **be regularly cleaned, disinfected, and cleared of parasites**. This means that keeping an eye on the illness, and preventing it from breaking out.

Pigeons are only rarely vaccinated against pox – usually those breeders use vaccines who have repeatedly struggled with the pox virus in the past. Every susceptible member of the flock in the loft **must be vaccinated at once**, and as early as possible, so that the longest possible time passes before the training period arrives and the racing season begins. The vaccination is of most value if young pigeons are already protected by the time the epidemic has its peak in the summer. The birds can be vaccinated **from the age of five weeks**.

Depending on the nature of the vaccine, the method of the vaccination can vary from the customary. With certain vaccines, we do not administer the liquid containing the live virus with a needle, but by **rubbing it into the feather follicles**. As a first step, a few feathers should be pulled out of the chest area, or rather, in the case of racing pigeons, from the side area of the leg. We should then apply the liquid containing an attenuated form of the virus onto the opened follicles where the feathers were pulled out, using a little brush, and with unidirectional movements. If follicles bleed after feathers are removed, we should find another point on the pigeon, because the blood flowing out neutralizes the vaccine virus, which thereby loses its effect.

If the vaccination is successful, then the empty follicles swell up a day or two afterwards, and after another few days the area begins to become scarred and scabbed. If these symptoms do not appear by about the seventh or tenth day, the vaccination has not "taken hold", and has failed. There can be a number of reasons for this, including the pigeon having a bad immune state, improper vaccination technique (bleeding), the birds being kept in inadequate conditions, or the specimen being transported or otherwise burdened in the meantime. These pigeons must be vaccinated all over again, once the inhibiting factor is overcome.

Note

If we use the above method to vaccinate a pigeon that has previously encountered the pox virus (either as a vaccine or through natural infection), the post-vaccination symptoms only appear as a mild rash, or not at all.

Infection with circovirus can ruin the effect of a vaccination against pox, and thus, as in the case of the vaccination against paramyxovirus, it is advisable to perform it as early as possible. If circovirus is present, or threatens to appear, it is best to perform the pox vaccination **when pigeons reach the age of five weeks**.

It is available as a **combined vaccine**, containing both paramyxovirus and pox virus. By using combined vaccines **we can save valuable weeks in the struggle against circovirus!**

Note

It is equally true in the pox case that it is forbidden to take pigeons to races, exhibitions, fairs, etc from an infected loft. We should not take them even if many or even most of the birds appear to be healthy, and do not (yet) display any of the symptoms of pigeon pox.

Pigeon herpes

The virus-induced pigeon herpes is primarily an illness affecting the **young age-group**. In more severe cases, it can lead to death in about 10% of infected birds.

Transmission

Adult pigeons carry the virus without displaying any symptoms, and do not normally develop any illness. Most often, the youngsters are already infected via crop milk, although antibodies acquired from the egg protect them from the illness in the first month or two of life by preventing the virus from multiplying. Thus the illness typically begins to appear after chicks are two months old, by which time antibodies received from the hen have run out.

At a later age, pigeons principally become infected when taken to races or exhibitions. On such occasions the virus attacks via the respiratory passages. If a pigeon is over six months in age and its immune state is average, the infection does not usually cause illness.

Damage

The virus that enters the body is usually only capable of "taking effect", that is multiplying and scattering from the point of infection, if the body is weakened for other reasons. Its characteristic points of attack are the respiratory passages, the liver, pancreas and the cells of the gut.

Symptoms

In acute cases we can observe **severe conjunctivitis**, and **strong, serous nasal discharge**, accompanied by inflammation of the throat. In most instances, symptoms in the upper respiratory passages are accompanied by diarrhoea. The ill birds are easily tired, do not move about, and in serious cases die within 3-4 days.

In more **prolonged** instances the virus also attacks the lower respiratory passages, the resulting symptom of which will be **heavy breathing**. In addition to the intestinal wall, the liver and pancreas are also damaged. If the damage to the liver and particularly to the pancreas is more significant, the ill pigeons quickly lose weight and then die.

Occasionally the virus also reaches the central nervous system, where it can cause encephalitis. This produces neurological symptoms like trembling and constrained motion.

Herpesvirus can pave the way for secondary attacks from other pathogens, most commonly mycoplasmas, salmonellas, and even trichomonads. The symptoms vary accordingly.

Pigeon herpes must be distinguished from:

- **paramyxovirus illness**, because of its neurological symptoms
- **haemophilus**, because of its symptoms in the area of the eyes
- **paratyphoid,** because of the diarrhoea, weight loss and neurological symptoms it causes
- **ornithosis**, because it can cause conjunctivitis and nasal discharge

Treatment

We can help the recovery of young pigeons with vitamins and immune boosters, and restrain secondary attacks from pathogens with the relevant medicines. If an older bird becomes ill with herpesvirus, this usually suggests serious problems with the immune system, and it is advisable to eliminate the specimen as quickly as possible.

Prevention

Before and during the breeding season, with the use of vitamins, amino acids and immune boosters we can ensure that the breeding-egg laid by the hen **contains as high a quantity of antibodies as possible**. The higher the level of antibodies at birth, the greater and more prolonged the protection given to nestlings from various infectious diseases.

3. Fungi-induced diseases

Fungi (mould fungi, conjugation fungi) can cause illnesses by entering the body directly, or via the poisons they produce, called fungal toxins or mycotoxins. Fungal infection can be symptom-free and go unnoticed, but toxicosis, poisoning that can cause mass death in pigeons, can also occur suddenly. Many species of fungi can cause disease, and the symptoms they cause can vary, as they can attack the lungs, the air sacs, the nervous system, the kidneys, etc. They can cause severe damage to the tissues of the **reproductive organs** (testicles, ovaries), which do not appear as direct symptoms; this can result in infertility or bad reproductivity.

Aflatoxicosis

The fungal poison aflatoxin is produced by the mould fungus Aspergillus flavus. It is in badly-stored feed or bedding that the fungi proliferate, especially when **the feed becomes wet, and is then stored in a warm place**. The fungal growth itself is often invisible, and the poison produced by the fungi can only be detected in a laboratory. That is, **seemingly healthy feed can cause fungal toxicosis** if it was previously not stored adequately.

Aflatoxin enters pigeons from feed or bedding. The toxin is capable of inducing serious illness or sudden death. It attacks almost all the organs, including the central nervous system, the lungs, the liver, the spleen, the kidneys, with different symptoms accordingly. Often, if the pigeons have only consumed a small amount of the poison, they can seem healthy at first glance, but, for example, turn out to be incapable of flying.

Fungal toxicosis is probably a much more common illness than it is diagnosed, as its variety of symptoms can be similar to those of many other infectious illnesses and poisonings. If we begin to suspect fungal toxicosis – **if many pigeons suddenly begin to display the same symptoms, or if there is frequent disgorging and/or rejection of feed** – we must carefully inspect the feed administered to the birds, and examine the conditions of its storage. If there is the slightest suspicion concerning the feed, we must stop giving it to the birds at once, and provide them with different feed that is properly stored and free of mould fungus.

Fungal toxins ruin the reproductive organs, **often causing infertility**. Typically it is feed that appears good, containing a small amount of toxin, that is the most dangerous from this point of view: organs do not display visible symptoms, but the amount of poison is nevertheless enough to destroy the sensitive tissue of the reproductive organs.

Aspergillosis

In the case of aspergillosis, it is **the fungus itself** (most commonly Aspergillus fumigatus) that enters the body, where it proliferates and causes illness. In one of its forms, a **button-like growth** develops in the upper part of the trachea, in the rear area of the throat, that obstructs breathing. This growth is **harder than that observed in the case of canker**, and its removal is difficult and painful, causing strong bleeding. Coughing and nasal discharge can also appear, which in further advanced cases is combined with diarrhoea, weight loss and even arthritis. The symptoms can be accompanied by conjunctivitis and significant lachrymation, but this is normally only seen in one eye.

The fungus also attacks the internal organs, causing necrotic inflammations in them. As there is little hope of complete recovery, **the best option is to put the ill bird down**, followed by repeated thorough cleaning and disinfection of the lofts and the surrounding area. If the pigeon in question is valuable, and the illness is only at the early stage, restricted to the buccal cavity, we can try to treat it, by repeatedly brushing the buccal cavity with diluted iodic solution (possibly mixed with honey). Experience shows that transmission within the loft is prevented by iodine and honey mixed into the drinking water (one teaspoon of iodic solution per five litres of water), but we should also note that it is easy to overdose iodine, poisoning the birds.

In the event of fungal infection, especially if it is humid and warm, the floor of the loft must be cleaned daily at all costs. Particular attention must be paid to ventilation, to prevent the humidity in the loft from increasing. We must protect the tissues of the pigeon's body with vitamins, especially **vitamin A**, and raise the operation of the immune system to the highest level, with immune stimulants. It is also important to assist the working of the liver with hepatoprotective agents.

Note

Antibiotics have no effect on fungi, and furthermore by repelling bacteria they undermine the body's necessary equilibrium between bacteria and fungi, giving the fungi even more room for manoeuvre. Thus **in cases** or suspected cases **of fungal illness**, **administering antibiotics is highly dangerous**

and forbidden, because it inevitably leads to exacerbation of the illness! Similarly, during antibiotics treatment we must not supply birds with yeast, as the otherwise innocent yeast organisms can overproliferate and attack the body.

Here we should note that artificial culturing of most pathogenic fungi is a simple, routine task, though they require slightly different conditions than bacteria do.

4. Parasite-induced diseases

Parasites are creatures that **feed off a host body**, causing damage by **siphoning off various forms of nutrition**. They can also **produce poisonous substances**, or **attack the tissues** of the host. In addition, they can cause **severe and continuous damage** by **spreading** other **pathogens**. We distinguish between external parasites (e.g. lice) and internal ones (e.g. roundworms).

Most parasites are multi-celled creatures, but there are also single-celled ones. The reason the latter cannot be listed among bacteria is that they are very different in terms of their cell structure, their way of life and their proliferation.

Intestinal worms

Hairworms, tapeworms and large roundworms can all settle in the intestines of pigeons.

About 20-30% of pigeons are infected with **large roundworms**. These worms live freely in the pigeon's intestinal system, sometimes in such numbers that they completely fill some of its sections. They primarily cause damage by siphoning off nutrients and producing poisonous substances, damage that can be fatal.

According to the statistics, there is a much higher proportion of infection with **hairworms** (small roundworms) in pigeons than with large roundworms. This can partly be explained by the fact that many other species of (wild) birds provide a home to pigeon hairworms, thus guaranteeing continual infection between species. Hairworms feed off their host by drilling their heads into the intestinal wall and clinging to it. They can cause serious damage to the intestinal wall, siphon off nutrients, and produce poisonous substances.

The incidence of tapeworms in pigeons is less significant.

Description

Large roundworms are colourless, one millimetre thick and a few centimetres long, and clearly visible to the naked eye. They generally reside in the upper section of the intestine, but in a case of severe infection they can fill almost the entire intestinal section. If they also appear in faeces released into the outside world, this is a sign of very severe infection. Their presence is most often revealed upon autopsy, when these worms can sometimes be found in the pigeon's intestines in great abundance.

Due to the nature of **hairworms** residing in the intestine, they are not released with faeces, but their thinness (their diameter is less than a tenth of a millimetre) makes it hard to see them, even on autopsy. Thus, despite their prevalence, their presence usually goes unnoticed, and maybe this helps explain why they are so widespread.

Tapeworms exist in many different shapes and sizes. It is common for them to use an intermediate host (e.g. an insect or a snail) in their reproductive cycle.

Damage, symptoms

Intestinal worms principally cause damage by siphoning off nutrients and by producing poisonous substances. If only a few worms are present, this is not significant, but if the infection is more severe, clinical symptoms can be observed. The ill pigeon **is dispirited, has no appetite, its plumage is ruffled, it has diarrhoea, and becomes thinner and thinner**. This thinness can become sickly, with muscles typically almost disappearing from the ill bird's breastbone. In the case of hairworm infection, the droppings can also be bloody, as these worms damage the intestinal tissues by drilling their heads into the intestinal wall.

For this reason, or because of the siphoning off of nutrients, the presence of worms over a prolonged period can cause **anaemia**.

Transmission

Adult worms residing in the intestine produce eggs in great numbers and on a continual basis, which, carried into the outside world in droppings, constantly infect the surrounding area. However, the released eggs require some weeks – **in a suitably damp and cool environment** – for the larva capable of infection to develop inside them. If one of these mature eggs gets inside the pigeon's intestinal system, the larva escapes from the egg and attaches itself to the intestinal wall. After a certain amount of time has passed, it turns into an adult worm, which siphons off nutrition from the host body all the while. When it becomes capable of reproduction, it begins producing and releasing eggs in its own right.

If the egg finds itself in an unfavourable, dry environment, it cannot begin its development into larva, but, as a result of its thick shell, **it can survive in the outside world for many years**, waiting for suitable conditions to emerge.

Eradication

It follows from the above that we cannot clear an infected flock of worms with a simple deworming procedure, as pigeons temporarily cleared of worms soon pick up the eggs present in large numbers in their environment, and the worms develop in their intestines again. **So the simultaneous destruction of the eggs in the environment is at least as important as deworming the birds**.

Destruction of the eggs

The eggs have thick, resistant shells, which once in the outside world defend them from dehydration; the **shell also provides effective protection** against various disinfectants. It is principally cleaning or rather **soaking** with **hot alkaline liquid** (bleach) that does them harm, but some are capable of surviving even this. There are breeders who swear that only fire has an effect on eggs in the cracks of the concrete floor of the loft. They perform this with a controllable open flame – of course only if the material of the cage makes this possible (i.e. if it is inflammable). This is a very dangerous method, which we do not recommend to anyone, but if someone does opt for it, fire and injury safety regulations must be adhered to in the strictest and most circumspect fashion!

If the base of the cage can be replaced (e.g. clay, sand, etc.), it is certainly advisable to remove the ground down to a depth of 20cm, and replace it with fresh, new material. The removed material is to be treated as biohazardous waste, and must be disposed of accordingly.

Deworming

There are many active ingredients in circulation against worms. Piperazine, previously popular, does not have an adequate effect, and a significant percentage of worms are not eliminated. **Tetramisole**, which is good against large roundworms, is more effective. Although in recent years there have been some reports of its effect declining, this is principally due to the fact that pigeons are not keen on drinking it because it is so bitter, and so often do not imbibe an adequate dose. **Levamisole** is more highly recommended, because it is less toxic and also has an immunostimulating effect. **Fenbendazole** and **mebendazole** have a broader deworming spectrum, as they are effective against tapeworms as well as large and small roundworms.

Ivermectin, a very effective drug against hairworms, is becoming more and more prevalent. It is also effective against large roundworms, but has no effect on tapeworms – though the latter only rarely cause problems in pigeon flocks. (It is effective, however, against arthropod parasites, which we will discuss later!) **Abamectin** is an even newer agent, and so is its mode of application: it is dripped onto the pigeon's skin. It is effective against external parasites and some internal ones, especially hairworms. **Moxidectin** is effective against large and small roundworms and external parasites. If it is necessary to treat pigeons during the period of rearing or racing, its low toxicity can make moxidectin the suitable choice.

When deworming, we must always treat **the entire flock**. Pigeons are not keen on consuming some products in their drinking water: many specimens would rather hardly drink anything for days than absorb the medicine mixed into it. Some other products are not soluble in water. For these reasons, it is advisable to administer most oral deworming agents **individually rather than in the flock's drinking water**, as this better guarantees that each pigeon receives enough of the medicine.

Microscopic examination of the pigeons' faeces is a fast and simple method of determining the current nature and quantity of the worm infection. It is advisable to make use of this, especially when the flock has already been infected with some kind of worm, for on such occasions it is exposed to the danger of direct infection for many years – thanks to the long survival period of the worm eggs.

Other internal worms

There are worms – of other species – that live not in the intestinal system but other parts of the pigeon's body. For example, some species of large and small roundworms settle in the windpipe, causing milder or more severe damage, principally respiratory symptoms. Fenbendazole, mebendazole and moxidectin are effective against these parasites outside the intestine, while ivermectin and abamectin primarily have an effect on hairworms. This means that by using these drugs our treatment of intestinal worms can in theory also clear pigeons of windpipe worms.

*

Unfortunately, not all animal breeders (not just pigeon breeders!) place adequate emphasis on deworming, even though regular eradication of parasites is not exclusively important because of the animals' health and performance. Humans and many species of animal "provide a home" for a high percentage of species of intestinal worm and external parasites, and so various internal and external worms can spread from one farm animal to another, from those to dogs and cats, and unfortunately to people, too. It is very important, therefore, that we subject our pigeons – just like any other animals kept around the house – to internal and external deworming **on a regular basis**. For intestinal worms, this must be done at least twice a year, after flying and before pairing, although it is better to eradicate them every three months.

Coccidiosis

It is coccidia, **single-celled parasites** that live inside the cells of the intestinal wall, that are responsible for the development of coccidiosis. They are capable of infecting many species of vertebrates, including pigeons. They can cause great damage for pigeon breeders as for breeders of other animals.

It is primarily the Eimeria colombanum and Eimeria labbeanna coccidia that cause disease in pigeons.

Transmission

Coccidiosis spreads through droppings, and in one particular respect its transmission is similar to that of intestinal worms. The offspring of these parasites, too, having left the host body and been released into the outside world in droppings, are present in a form that is **not yet infectious**. In order for them to infect another pigeon orally, they have to undergo a maturation (sporulation) in the outside world lasting a few days. For this maturation they require a damp, warm environment. (The ideal for them is 28 degrees Celsius, at which their transformation can take place within as little as two days.) So, if the infected faeces finds itself in such a place for a few days, infectious coccidia develop in it which can then cause illness in pigeons that absorb them.

Damage

Like many other microorganisms, coccidia do not cause disease if they are only present in the system in small quantities. On such occasions the body's immune system "reins in" the alien creatures within the body, keeping them in equilibrium with the host. But if for some reason the immune system is weakened (e.g. due to a high level of stress), or the microorganisms enter the body in too high a quantity, the equilibrium is upset and the first symptoms begin to appear.

The coccidia attack the cells of the intestinal wall, proliferate inside them, then, once the cell is destroyed, the freed pathogens begin to target new cells. Intestinal inflammation occurs, and the mucosa and deeper layers of the intestinal wall are damaged, which can lead to worsening diarrhoea. The watery faeces will be greeny-brown; afterwards it can become distinctly sanguineous.

Coccidiosis can affect pigeons of any age, but it usually inflicts the greatest damage on **weaned young birds**. Its effect can open the door for many other pathogens, meaning that diseases can worsen and vary within the loft.

Symptoms

One fairly common symptom of coccidiosis is **droppings** that are phlegmatous-aqueous, often **turning** greeny-brown, then **sanguineous**, though we should add that sometimes salmonellas or hairworms can produce bloody faeces. Diarrhoea is accompanied by dispiritedness; the pigeons "**mope around**", their plumage is ruffled. Their consumption of feed decreases dramatically, while their water intake increases. Specimens displaying severe symptoms soon die.

During autopsy, along various sections of the intestinal wall we can see an inflamed mucous membrane imbibed with blood. The contents of the gut have a characteristic smell, and even in recently perished bodies we can often find sections of the intestine that are full of gas.

Treatment

Certain sulfonamide derivatives are well-established as effective against coccidia, though just as in the case of bacteria, we can encounter resistance to certain drugs. We can also use **sulfadimethoxine, sulfachlorpyrazine** or sulfaquinoxalin, each combined with trimethoprim.

Amprolium derivatives are also effective – they act by inhibiting the effect of vitamin B1. For this reason we should **not** administer vitamin mixtures containing vitamin B1 to the pigeons during their use. While using them (as a result of the relative B1 deficiency that develops) the treated pigeons can be lethargic, dispirited, and so we should not use them during racing season.

One of the most popular drugs around the world is **toltrazuril**.

Treatment generally lasts for three to five days, depending on the product used. Following the treatment, we should give the pigeons a vitamin mixture, and not forget that the medication may have significantly decreased the amount of normal intestinal bacteria, and so these should also be restored.

Prevention

Coccidia forms released with droppings are only capable of developing into infectious structures if they remain in a damp, warm environment once in the outside world. This means that **regular cleaning of the cage** is important, something we should pay even greater attention to in damp, humid weather. If the floor of the cage is damp and dries with difficulty, we should scatter adsorbent material on it, like zeolite.

Note

A small number of coccidia in the pigeon's body does not cause illness, indeed their presence can even be advantageous for its resistance, as it keeps the immune system in check. The reverse is also true: if microscopic examination only reveals a low number of parasites in faeces, this is probably a sign that the pigeon's immune system is working well. From this it follows that a large increase in the number of coccidia in droppings shows that the pigeon's resistance is weakened: we should be prepared for some other pathogen to attack the pigeon, or perhaps it has already done so (e.g. circovirus).

Canker (Trichomoniasis)

Trichomoniasis, better known as "canker", is caused by Trichomonas gallinae. It is a single-celled flagellate parasite capable of independent movement. It is prevalent around the world, and is capable of causing huge losses for fanciers. It has a very high reproductive capacity, and can also attack the pigeons' vital organs.

Adult pigeons usually carry the parasite without displaying any symptoms, but weakened specimens and particularly **young birds** can suffer severe, sometimes fatal diseases.

Transmission

The majority of adult pigeons are infected with the pathogen, but – if their immune systems are strong – they carry this single-celled parasite without displaying any symptoms. Trichomonad hides itself in the mucosa of the throat, the oesophagus, and the crop, residing there in small numbers without causing symptoms.

The infected specimens (even those with no symptoms!) release the pathogen in saliva and faeces, which then infects orally. Young pigeons are typically infected either orally by their parents **via crop milk**, or through a navel that has not healed. Amongst specimens in other age-groups it is infected drinking water that is the primary mode of transmission, but the pathogen can also be passed on in droppings.

Damage

The pathogen can cause local alterations to the mucosa of the **throat**, and can also spread in the digestive tract and the whole of the body. In young birds it can reside in the area of the **navel** which has not yet retreated, going on to reach the liver, the lungs and other internal organs.

Symptoms

Clinical symptoms do not develop in older pigeons carrying the parasite if their immune system is working properly. Often it is only a **decline in flying performance** that suggests that a pigeon is infected with trichomonad; we may observe birds being a little out of breath after they land. As a result of the stress of transportation and racing, the latent illness can flare up, or open a path for other pathogens.

There are **two main forms** in which the illness appears in young pigeons or weakened adult specimens; in nestlings there is also a third form that can appear, in which the navel is inflamed.

Buccal form

One key symptom in the buccal cavity is a **yellow, button-like form, cheesy in consistency**, which gave rise to the everyday name for the disease (canker). There are local alterations even before the yellow form appears, but these normally escape the breeder's attention. By this time the mucous membrane of the throat has turned red, and a phlegmatous deposit appears on it.

Consumption of feed becomes a challenge for ill birds, and so it declines. Intake of drinking water usually increases at first, but later, as a result of greater deposits, **drinking** also becomes difficult, and the level of water consumed can fall. Respiratory problems can also appear.

Inflammation of the navel

This is an illness that exclusively affects **young specimens that are only a few days old**; they are infected directly from the infected nest through an unclosed navel. In this instance a characteristic, cheesy abscess-like deposit develops under the skin in the area of the navel. The pathogen is further transmitted from here, affecting internal organs, which can often result in a quick death.

Illness of internal organs

The characteristic yellowy-cheesy changes most often develop in the liver, destroying the liver tissue once they penetrate deeply. In young specimens, a **watery**, **typically strong-smelling diarrhoea** can appear **after two weeks of life**, and the symptoms of stunted development soon become clear. This form can also occur in adults, accompanied by loss of weight, with the ill birds **dispirited**, **becoming thin**, "going light". A yellowy-coloured diarrhoea can also develop, which can be accompanied by abdominal puffiness. In chronic cases, the whites of the eyes, the conjunctiva, and occasionally the whole of the skin can take on a yellowish shade.

Diagnosis of the illness when the typical alterations appear is not usually very difficult, and, in addition, with microscopic examination of samples taken from the relevant place (throat, crop), the pathogens can be detected directly. We note that a smear-test of the crop milk of adult birds not displaying symptoms generally gives a positive result. We can only prepare for an outbreak of the disease if the number of pathogens present in the examined sample rises above a certain level.

Treatment

The yellowy-cheesy substance in the throat can easily be **removed** with the help of a cotton bud (Q-Tip). We should brush the place of the removed button with diluted iodic solution.

There are a number of agents around the world for the treatment and prevention of the illness, but whether they are accessible or on a ban list depends on the country in question.

In some countries medicines based on **dimetridazole** are in circulation, which is allowed in Europe, Australia and Canada, but a banned ingredient in the USA. (It is important to note that it can only be administered to sport animals and pets, and **must not be given to those bred for their meat!**)

Ronidazole is available in many places in Europe and Australia. **Carnidazole** is the agent sold in the USA. Breeders use human products containing **metronidazole** all over the world.

If a number of products are available, it is advisable to alternate them after a given period. If we administer one drug for too long, we can expect its effect to diminish after a while.

The **treatment** of canker should take place **for three to five consecutive days**, but in severe instances may require seven days. Bearing in mind the prevalence of the pathogen and its highly contagious nature, we should treat **the whole of the flock**. Antibiotics may also be used, as bacteria can be part of the damage caused by canker. Antibiotic treatment must be carefully considered and targeted, however, to avoid placing an unnecessary burden on the body. This is very important, as **the liver may already be damaged** as a result of the direct attack of the pathogen, and the medicines against trichomonads (primarily dimetridazole) themselves represent an extra burden, especially on the liver. For all these reasons, the tolerance of the bird's system is stretched to its limits, and an antibiotic that is the wrong type or administered in the wrong dose can easily lead to death.

During and immediately after the treatment we should take care to ensure suitable provision of vitamins and **active protection of the liver**.

*

Manufacturers generally state the dosage of medicine for canker relative to a quantity of drinking water (e.g. 2 grams per litre). But if because of hot weather, or for other reasons (e.g. in the breeding season), the daily water intake increases, we must be careful not to overdose the medicine, for this can cause poisoning symptoms, and, in the case of severe overdose, even death! To avoid this, we should always only prepare the amount of medicated water that our birds drink on an average day. Then, if it happens to be a hot day, and the medicated water runs out, we should only give the flock ordinary water for the rest of the day.

Example. The average intake of water in the loft is five litres. In hot weather this can easily rise to double that, i.e. 10 litres. If we were to mix two grams into each litre of water, the pigeons would be given twice the prescribed dose on that day, which is not just a waste of money, but is also a heavy burden on their bodies (which are in any case under considerable stress from the heat!). So we should calculate the daily dose of medicine, with is 5 x 2 grams, i.e. 10 grams, mix this into 5 litres of water, then when this has run out completely, we should only give them untreated water. (It is not a good solution to mix the daily dosage (10 grams) into 10 litres of water, because then it becomes too diluted and loses its effectiveness, and also it would stand in the water for too long, which in hot weather can mean it breaks down quickly.)

On a stiflingly hot day, however, we must further "fine-tune" this method, because our pigeons, in the sweltering heat, would drink up all the medicated water within an hour or two, which is unsafe. On such a hot day, therefore, the daily dose should be divided into two parts, and given to the pigeons in the morning and in the evening, or we should schedule the treatment during the period(s) of the day when the temperature is not at its peak.

As long as there is medicated water within reach of the pigeons, they must not be allowed access to other sources of water, e.g. bathing water.

Note

Agents that are hardly or not soluble (e.g. pure metronidazole) must of course be administered on an individual basis.

Prevention

As the pathogen is extremely widespread and highly contagious, regular medical prevention must be used against it. The rules of this must be adhered to in order for us not to produce strains of pathogen that are resistant to medicines.

Preventive treatment is associated with two main periods, the racing season and pairing.

As far as the racing season is concerned, many recommend two main preventive treatments: one before the racing season, and another one immediately after it. On both occasions we administer the medicine over five days. (In the course of the racing season we can also perform shorter treatments every two, three or four weeks. These preventive treatments should last for **at least three days**. This allows prevention or at least delay of the development of resistance to the medicine, something that is unfortunately increasingly evident in the case of trichomonads.)

The period of treatment around the time of **pairing** should also be at least five days. The treatment should take place **before pairing**. If this fails to happen, it must be done after eggs are laid but before chicks hatch.

External parasites

These parasites are widely prevalent. They belong to the group of arthropods: they include insects, e.g. bird lice, or arachnids, like mites or ticks.

Damage

The damage caused by external parasites can be divided into three components. Firstly, their presence **bothers** the host animal, which above a certain level can act as an outright stress factor. Secondly, as a result of their parasitical way of life, they **take nutrition away** from the host body, and/or **damage the plumage**: this includes those that are specifically blood-suckers, those that consume the material of the feathers or the cells of the skin's epithelium, and creatures that are a mix of both. Thirdly, they can be **vectors** for **other illnesses**, e.g. **paratyphoid and pox**.

Symptoms

In general, we can say that pigeons infected with external parasites are nervous, their performance declines, and they succumb to a variety of illnesses more quickly. In addition to these general characteristics, more specific symptoms develop as a result of the typical nutrition of particular parasites.

Blood-suckers siphon off nutrition directly from the host body. This can go as far as the host animal falling ill, displaying rather uncharacteristic symptoms. Initially it is only the performance of the pigeon which is worse than usual, but later it can also lose weight, which is accompanied by **anaemia**. The pigeon tires easily and is bad-tempered. All these symptoms are worsened by secondary illnesses. The younger age-group reacts more sensitively to these parasites, too: a severe infection can even cause a high level of death amongst them.

Plumage damagers cause disorders in the growth of feathers, but also destroy the stock of already developed feathers. The pigeon's plumage is incomplete, scraggy; certain feathers will be deformed. All this is at serious cost to flying performance.

(In addition, special symptoms can also appear, e.g. respiratory problems caused by the damage of mites residing internally on the air-sacs.)

Way of life

The life of external parasites varies, and we must be aware of this for prevention to be successful. Some of them (e.g. itch-mites living in the skin, or feather lice) spend their entire lives on the host body, while others (e.g. blood-sucking lice) only visit their prey to feed (usually at night), **hiding in the surroundings** for the large part of the day.

Prevention and treatment

The precise determination of the types of the various external parasites first takes place with a thorough visual inspection, for which it does no harm to use a magnifying glass. Certain parasites (e.g. itch-mites) are not visible even like this, and so there is often need for additional techniques, like the microscopic examination of scraps of skin or parts of feathers. In the search for parasites we must examine the whole surface of the pigeon's body, as different species have a penchant for residing in different areas of the body (e.g. scaly mites in the skin of the feet).

Prevention is made easier by the fact that most antiparasitic drugs have an effect on all external parasites. Just as in the case of intestinal worms, we require **treatment of the flock** here, too, and it is also **necessary to rid the surroundings** of parasites. The latter refers to the eggs laid down by the parasites, but also to the developed blood-suckers which spend the majority of their time hidden in the surrounding area.

Elimination of parasites has to be combined with a big spring clean, i.e. finding and removing the hiding places of parasites and their eggs. This can be followed by an efficient method of disinfection, which is not without its effect on other pathogens (e.g. bacteria) as well. Finally, the building of the loft and pieces of furniture must be sprayed or washed with special antiparasitic substances.

We can treat the pigeons themselves by bathing them, or by spraying or dusting them individually: this means the antiparasitic substances are applied directly to the surface of the (whole) body. Drugs for individual treatment include **transmix**, **tetramethrin**, **permethrin** and **bioresmethrin**. In addition we can use products containing **ivermectin**, which we use internally (dripping into the mouth), because after being absorbed their effect also spreads to external parasites (and to some internal worms). The latest products to arrive on the market are ones that are **dripped onto the skin**, like **abamectin**, which is also effective against the majority of both external and internal parasites.

Even after successful elimination of parasites we cannot sit on our laurels, however. Their widespread presence means that the loft can become reinfected at any time, and so regular and continuous inspection of pigeons for them is vital. Their strong prevalence means that preventive treatment is recommended on at least two occasions a year, one of which should be timed to fall in the weeks before pairing.

Note

During the incubation period we should not spray nests with a strong-smelling product, because pigeons may abandon their eggs (possibly for ever)!

Important!

Antiparasitic products for external use on other species of animal (e.g. with **diazinone** as their active ingredient) can be deathly **poisonous** to pigeons, and so we must be very careful when selecting the product we use, and ask the advice of a professional! There have been many occasions where breeders have "succeeded" in eradicating the entire pigeon flock as well as the parasites by using an incorrectly chosen product!

You can see Table 2 and Table 3 at the very end of the book:
Table 2. Comparison of the symptoms of contagious diseases
Young age group

Table 3. Comparison of the symptoms of contagious diseases
Older age group

Metabolic diseases

A wide variety of organic and inorganic compounds need to be consumed for an animal's body to operate properly. The body processes these substances arriving from the outside world via very complicated methods, gains energy from them, assimilates them, and discharges parts that are unnecessary or possibly damaging.

One group of metabolic illnesses is those that occur if the body **is not provided with adequate** amounts of some organic or inorganic substance. We refer to this as **deficiency illness**. It also has a negative effect on the metabolism if **too high an amount** of some substance enters the body at once: this can lead to minor or more severe **poisoning**.

1. Deficiency illnesses

By **absolute deficiency** we mean that an inadequate amount of the missing substance is present in a body operating in an average fashion.

Relative deficiency is when the body's requirement for a certain substance increases as a result of some factor (e.g. stress), or if (because of some illness) the absorption or processing of that substance **becomes disturbed**. On such occasions the normal level of the substance proves inadequate, and insufficiency disease develops in the same way.

Absolute and relative deficiencies may display the same symptoms. The primary difference, however, is that all fanciers consciously try to prevent absolute deficiency illnesses by the continuous administering of vitamins, amino acids and mineral supplements. But only few breeders **also pay attention to the possibility of relative deficiencies**, for example in the case of a longer period of stress or an infectious disease.

In the following sections we list the most important groups of organic and inorganic substances which the pigeon's body is continuously in need of, the inadequate intake of which often causes functional anomalies or illness.

Vitamins

Vitamins, which are needed in the course of metabolic processes, are indispensable compounds for animals and human beings. Pigeons either receive vitamins directly as part of their feed, or acquire them in the form of so-called pre-vitamins, which turn into efficient vitamins inside the body.

We list vitamins in two main groups. They are those that are soluble in fat – vitamins A, D, E and K. The most common vitamins that are soluble in water are B1, B2, B3, B6 and B12, biotin, folic acid and vitamin C.

The body is capable of storing vitamins that are soluble in fat, and so a deficiency in these develops more slowly, which, on the other hand, makes it all the easier to overdose them, especially vitamins A and D. Water-soluble vitamins are quickly released with urine, and so a deficiency can appear more quickly, but overdosing involves less risk (as the surplus is soon eliminated by the system).

The body's vitamin requirements vary. It requires a certain amount at all points of its life, but needs more than average **at a young age**, during **growth**, **moulting**, **pairing**, **rearing of chicks**, as well as **during and after illnesses**. The need for certain vitamins typically increases under significant **physical burdens** (racing) and particularly under **stress**.

In pigeon-breeding, we regularly give vitamins to prevent vitamin deficiency from developing. We must be aware that for the above reasons the requirements can increase, even to a high degree, and the dose must be raised accordingly.

Inadequate intake or absence of vitamins can lead to the development of severe illnesses, which, naturally, can be prevented or treated with a dosage of the appropriate vitamin. An overdose of fat-soluble vitamins can also create problems, and so we must observe the recommended dosage and our veterinarian's advice when administering them.

Absorption varies from one vitamin to the next. Water-soluble ones are easily absorbed through the intestinal wall, while those soluble in fat are only effective if fats and oils are also present in the contents of the gut, which help their absorption. For this reason, a deficiency of fat-soluble vitamins can develop even if an adequate amount is mixed into the drinking water but the **consumption of feed** is insufficient, or if the nutrition does not contain enough vegetable oil. We note that disturbance in the body's fat metabolism – when **the liver is damaged** as a result of an antibiotics overdose, for example – can also lead to a deficiency in fat-soluble vitamins.

*

The following are the most important vitamins for pigeons:

Vitamin A

A fat-soluble vitamin originating from the carotenes found in plants. It is essential for the health of the epithelial tissue of the **skin** and for growth of the **bones**, and also plays a very important role in **vision**. Its pre-vitamin **carotene is of key importance in reproductive processes**; a lack of it leads to a decline in propensity for pairing, and infertility of eggs.

It is primarily green plant parts that contain carotene, while vitamin A itself is to be found in larger quantities in animal tissue (especially in the liver – cod-liver oil). As pigeons consume little green food, carotene and vitamin A deficiency can easily develop, and supplements must be administered on a regular basis. The intake of vitamin A is particularly important in the case of illnesses attacking the epithelium, like **pox**. On such occasions we should administer vitamin mixtures containing vitamin A in large (but not too large) doses.

If **reproductive disorders** appear, it is certainly advisable to give carotene as well as vitamin A, especially if these are connected to problems with the operation of the liver (e.g. because of an antibiotics overdose). This is also important because the breeding season of pigeons is restricted to early spring, when the carotene content of feed is at its lowest, and so its intake is low to begin with! The dosage of carotene and vitamin A is particularly important if the flock was treated with antibiotics in the period before pairing. The adverse effect of antibiotics on the operation of the liver only serves to increase the need for carotene and vitamin A, which is already heightened during this period (relative deficiency!). It may be that **the infertility of eggs** can be traced back to **the relative lack of carotene** in many more instances than we might expect.

B vitamins

These vitamins are soluble in water, and therefore must be administered on a daily basis. The members of this group of vitamins play a role in a wide variety of metabolic processes, and so a shortage of them can manifest itself in many different symptoms. An insufficient intake leads to general **dispiritedness**, **weight loss**, a **combination of neurological symptoms**, and **a tendency to illness**.

Whole (unhusked) seeds of cereals contain them in large quantities, and so the pigeons' daily requirement is usually guaranteed. If for some reason the consumption of feed declines or stops, or the body's vitamin B requirement increases as a result of some illness, it is essential that pigeons be given B vitamins in their water, or in more severe cases by injection.

Some medicines against coccidiosis contain amprolium, which has the effect of expelling vitamin B1. Amprolium blocks the operation of vitamin B1 in the whole body of the pigeon, not just in the coccidia, thereby causing dispiritedness and exhaustion. Therefore we must **not** use medicines containing amprolium **before races and exhibitions**!

Vitamin C

A water-soluble vitamin that can be damaging if heavily overdosed, as it can produce uroliths in the kidneys. It is the most significant **anti-stress** vitamin. Though the pigeon's system is capable of producing it on its own, under heavy stress the body's vitamin C requirement increases greatly, and substitute intake may be required. With continual daily dosage we can efficiently decrease the harmful effects of stress. It is primarily recommended **in very hot weather, or during lengthy transportation or illness**.

One very significant characteristic of vitamin C is that it helps the body to neutralize and expel toxic, poisonous substances. As most antibiotics are toxic for the system, it is useful – especially in the case of a longer course of antibiotics – to complement them with vitamin C therapy. (It must not be administered together with gentamycin.)

If there is a prolonged burden on the skeletal muscle, the relative lack of oxygen means that after a while lactic acid inevitably develops in the muscle cells, which also has a toxic, cell-damaging effect. Vitamin C aids the removal of the lactic acid from the muscle cells before it causes greater damage. For this reason, it is very effective if administered **before races** and immediately **after arrival**.

Vitamin D

Fat-soluble vitamin. The skin is capable of producing vitamin D from its pre-vitamin substances in response to sunlight, but if necessary the vitamin can also be administered in ready-made form. Its most important role is in **the regulation of calcium (lime) and the associated phosphoric metabolism**.

A lack of vitamin D principally causes ossification disorders (rickets). Hens' vitamin D requirements increase during the breeding season, when they may be a need for it to be administered on a systematic basis. As in the absence of vitamin D calcium is not adequately absorbed from the gut, we cannot effectively prevent osteomalacia and eggshell deficiency (paper eggshells) by the application of lime feed alone.

Overdose of vitamin D **is also dangerous**, as it can cause bone fragility and general calcification of the tissues, inducing locomotor disorders, for example.

Vitamin E

A fat-soluble vitamin. Found in large quantities in vegetable oils and seeds, but mouldy or rancid feed can lose its vitamin E content, or the intake of such feed can multiply the body's vitamin E requirements.

If the vitamin is insufficient or absent (especially if the specimen also suffers from selenium deficiency), **dystrophy of the heart muscle and skeletal muscle** occurs, which is particularly damaging for racing pigeons. It also has a very important role in **reproduction**, and stock birds – males and females – cannot be without it for healthy spermatogenesis. In its absence the number of infertile eggs increases, which can be aggravated by a decline in propensity for pairing.

Vitamin K

One of the fat-soluble vitamins, but not one that is stored in the system. It is necessary for healthy **operation of the liver** and **blood coagulation**. Normal intestinal flora produces it on a continuous basis, and so there is rarely a shortage of it. If the intestinal flora is chronically restricted, damaged or destroyed, however (e.g. after a course of antibiotics), then a vitamin K deficiency can appear, which causes disorders in liver operation and blood clotting. (As antibiotics represent a burden on the liver in and of themselves, which is only aggravated by the lack of vitamin K caused by the destruction of intestinal bacteria, overly frequent doses of antibiotics do more harm than good.)

The majority of rat and mouse poisons contains a dicumarol-like compound which suspends the effects of vitamin K: as a result of blood coagulation disorder, the poisoned bird bleeds to death a few days after it consumes the poison. For this reason, if our pigeons happen accidentally to consume **mouse or rat killer**, we should consult a veterinarian at once – deaths can be prevented by administering a vitamin K antidote, if begun in good time and done by an expert.

Macro elements

Macro elements are what we call the elements and mineral constituents that the body requires in relatively large quantities.

In the case of pigeons it is principally the absence or overdose of calcium, phosphor and magnesium that cause problems.

Calcium

An element belonging to the alkaline earth metals. We encounter it in everyday pigeon-breeding in the form of lime feed (calcium carbonate), sea shells, bone flour, etc. Its physiological role is extensive, and the body needs it in large quantities. It plays an important role in bone and eggshell formation, which is why a pigeon's calcium requirements are greatest when young and when laying eggs. It plays a role in the operation of the nervous system, and is essential for the normal operation of heart, skeletal and smooth muscles.

Its absence in young birds manifests itself in ossificational difficulties, in the softening and deformation of bones. In adults a shortage of it is evident from a decline in flying performance, from the laying of eggs with soft shells, and, in worse cases, from a decline in the number of eggs. If its intake is inadequate, the propensity for inflammation increases, and coagulation disorders can emerge.

Pigeons need a continuous intake of calcium. This takes place in the form of various mineral substance mixtures, but we must pay attention to the fact that without vitamin D the body has problems **absorbing** the calcium from the gut properly, and so, particularly in winter and early spring when there is little light, products with lime should be accompanied with vitamin mixtures including vitamin D.

Magnesium

Magnesium, like calcium a member of the alkaline earth metals, has an important role in normal ossification processes and in the operation of the nervous system. It is also essential for keeping the immune system at a high level.

The principal consequences of a shortage of magnesium are ossification disorders and signal transduction problems. The pigeons' performance declines, and their propensity for developing tumours increases.

Its everyday formulation is Epsom salt. Administered orally, it has a laxative effect. In smaller quantities it can be used to **increase the appetite**.

A shortage of magnesium is rare, but in the case of prolonged stress or a heavy burden on the system, there may be a need for it to be supplemented.

Phosphor

In its free forms this element is highly poisonous, but in compound form it is essential for the operation of the living organism. It is necessary for the development of bones and feathers, the normal operation of nerve cells, and it has a very significant role in cell division, and thereby also in reproduction.

If it is absent, there are disorders in the development of the skeleton and plumage, and neurological problems can also appear. Chronic lack of phosphor causes growth deficiency and emaciation. If the supply of phosphor is insufficient, we should not expect good **reproduction** statistics!

The body's phosphor requirement is highest at a young age and during the breeding season. There may be a need for an increased intake of phosphor during **convalescence** after an illness (this is particularly effective if **combined with vitamin B12**).

Overdosage

It is not the overdose of the macro element *per se* that causes damage, as the exaggerated quantity of the element is not absorbed from the intestine, but is simply released from the system. (Naturally this only holds for doses administered orally. If we give an overdose of some macro element in injection form, we can cause severe metabolic illness, indeed a speedy death.) The overdose of the macro element causes damage because it **blocks the absorption of other elements**, leading to the associated deficiency illnesses. Thus, for example, too high a dose of calcium can interfere with the absorption of both magnesium and phosphor from the gut, and thereby with the healthy proportion of these elements in the body's metabolism.

We draw the reader's attention to the fact that nutrition supplements containing calcium (lime) neutralize certain antibiotics (tetracycline derivatives, gentamycin), thus rendering them ineffective, and so we should avoid administering them together.

Micro elements, trace elements

Micro elements and trace elements are so called because, relative to the other elements, they are only present in small or very small quantities in living organisms. This does not mean that they are not just as vital for normal life; an inadequate amount of them can lead to disease, and their total absence to death.

The most important micro and trace elements in pigeon care are (with the element's chemical symbol in brackets): selenium (Se), manganese (Mn), molybdenum (Mo), copper (Cu), boron (B), chromium (Cr), zinc (Zn), nickel (Ni) and vanadium (V).

In principle, the pigeons' feed should contain adequate quantities of these micro and trace elements. A deficiency illness can appear, however, if we give the birds the same feed for too long a period, or if provision of feed is good but some chronic, prolonged disease worsens the absorption of micro elements (e.g. because of intestinal inflammation) or the entry of elements into the metabolic cycle (e.g. because of liver damage). On such occasions microelements should be added to the feed in the form of supplements or additives.

Plants grown on land that is only treated with artificial fertilizers contain inadequate levels of some micro elements, as the fertilizers, unlike organic compost, do not contain micro elements, and indeed they block them from being absorbed by roots. As most fanciers give their pigeons feed that from this perspective is of unknown origin, they must reckon with the possibility that the nutritional values even of seemingly perfect feed can be inadequate. So it is advisable to add supplements containing micro and trace elements to the feed **at regular intervals**.

In some periods, the body's needs for trace and micro elements increases. These periods are typically when birds are young, and the breeding months. The reproductive organs are particularly sensitive to the absence of particular micro and trace elements: if there is even a slight shortage of these in the body, the stock bird appears entirely healthy, but **the flock's reproduction and fertility parameters decline**.

*

In pigeon-breeding it is selenium deficiency that we encounter the most often, and so we discuss this in more detail.

Selenium

In many countries the earth is not usually rich in selenium, and so plants grown in it only contain this element in minimal quantities. The utilization of the low selenium content of the soil is further worsened by artificial fertilizers, and so in such regions a shortage of selenium in animal (and human) bodies can easily appear. All the more so because drinking water in these areas tends to have little or no selenium in it.

An inadequate quantity of selenium causes disorders in the operation of the **immune system**, and in worse cases can lead to **hepatic dystrophy**. In racing pigeons even a small shortage can have very serious consequences, as an insufficient level of selenium can lead to **skeletal and heart muscle dystrophy**, which on the one hand seriously weakens flying performance, and on the other hand the damage to the heart can mean that a single heavier load placed on the body can quickly lead to death.

A bird's selenium requirement is high when young, and an inadequate intake causes developmental disorders and slow growth. The role selenium plays in **reproduction** is also very important – if we do not ensure its regular intake, especially in the winter and the spring, reproductive disorders can develop.

The presence of selenium is also required for the connective tissues of the motor organs, the tendons, ligaments, and particularly the cartilages, to be suitably flexible and resistant.

Selenium is easily and quickly absorbed from the gut, and so administering it orally is an entirely suitable method. (We normally give selenium **together with vitamin E**.) Its regular intake is necessary, but this does **not** mean that it should be administered **on a continuous basis**, as **selenium is easy to overdose**! A heavy overdose can cause poisoning, liver damage, and in severe cases even death. So supplements of selenium should only continuously be administered for a week at most, after which we should have a one or two week break. This is the treatment to be used if the lack of selenium is already established. **One supplement of selenium per week is adequate as a preventive measure**, but it is advisable to continue this regularly, throughout the year.

Proteins, amino acids

Proteins are huge molecules that are made up of smaller ones, so-called amino acids. The body first breaks down the plant and animal protein consumed with feed into these constituent elements, then builds up its own body proteins from them.

The pigeons' protein molecules are built up from twenty-two different amino acids. The body is capable of producing the majority of these itself, but there are ten amino acids it needs to consume in a ready form – we call these **essential amino acids**. The more a type of nutrition contains these essential amino acids, the higher its protein value. It is important for us to be aware that the production of the body's own proteins is determined by the amino acid that is present in the smallest quantity; that is to say, the absence or decreased amount of a single essential amino acid is enough for the body's protein metabolism to suffer disorders. And the direct consequences of this are a decline in flying performance and damage to the immune system.

The extent to which the different types of feed contain essential amino acids varies – sweetcorn, for example, contains only scant amounts of the amino acids lysine and tryptophan. So birds kept on a solitary diet of sweetcorn soon suffer disorders in their protein metabolism.

During races, the breast musculature of the pigeon contracts nine or ten times a second, for many hours at a time. This enormous burden, or rather strain, inevitably leads to some level of damage to the breast musculature. The regeneration of the musculature can be assisted by an intake of amino acids, among other things, which it is advisable to begin as soon as the pigeons return home. All the more so because we slightly lowered the protein content of feed before the pigeons were caged up.

There are also times outside the racing season when supplementary intake of amino acids can be required. These include the moulting season, periods of great heat and other stressors, youth, and when rearing the young. Pigeons that are ill for any reason generally need a heightened amino acid intake. It is important that we ensure special sources of essential amino acids in these periods. For this reason, it is best to use vitamin mixtures that also contain essential amino acids.

2. Poisonings

A large number of substances can cause poisoning in pigeons, and as a result **the symptoms of poisoning can vary widely**. All the more so as this includes poisonings caused by the fancier himself, when the dosage of some medicine exceeds the body's tolerance level.

We should suspect poisoning if **suddenly or within a short period many of our pigeons**, perhaps the whole flock, fall ill, and the birds display **identical or highly similar symptoms**. **Neurological symptoms** are common: a heightened nervous state, or quite the opposite, lethargy and sedentariness. **Vomiting and/or diarrhoea also appear often, but sudden, possibly**

large-scale death of birds can also occur, without any prior symptoms.

If we suspect poisoning, our first task is immediately **to remove the drinking and bathing water** currently laid out for the pigeons, **as well as all their feed**, and **provide clean water instead**. After this, we strive to find out the cause of the poisoning, taking all the possibilities into consideration, e.g. whether we have administered any medicine, whether the pigeons have been out in the yard, where they might have eaten mushrooms, sprayed or poisonous plants, whether we have sprinkled or bathed them with something ourselves, whether they can have come into contact with rat poison, whether the feed has been changed, etc.

If we suspect poisoning, the most important thing is **to identify the poison**, because the fate of the poisoned pigeons largely depends on this. For the majority of poisons there are antidotes, or at least methods by which the damage they cause can be decreased. Ordering and using these requires specialist veterinary knowledge, but **the speedy identification of the poison is** largely **up to the fancier**. If this is not successful, we can expect the worst.

We should note that the treatment of the poisoned pigeons – as it generally takes place individually and over a prolonged period – is expensive and tiring work, the results of which are often uncertain. In addition, even if the pigeon survives the poisoning, it can suffer such irreversible damage (muscle degradation, damage to reproductive organs) that it becomes worthless. In the case of poisonings, as elsewhere, the best policy is prevention.

Poisonings caused by medicines

Most often, there are two reasons that occur for poisonings. One is an overdose of dimetridazole; the other is an exceeded dose of one or more antibiotics.

Poisonings caused by **dimetridazole** (used against canker) and similar compounds typically occur in very hot weather. Water consumption can rise to many times the usual level, and if the fancier measures out medicine based on the level of water consumed at that moment (putting the prescribed amount in each litre), he can easily give the birds an overdose. To prevent this, **the daily amount of medicine should always be calculated based on water consumption on an average day**, and this is how much should be added to drinking water. (See the section entitled "Canker – Trichomoniasis" for more details.)

The overdose of dimetridazole causes neurological symptoms: the pigeons stagger about dizzily, and collapse. Vomiting can also occur, which is fortunate, as the body thereby relieves itself of a part of the poisonous substance. If too much poison is absorbed, the pigeon dies from the damage to the nervous system and the liver.

Treatment

As soon as symptoms of poisoning appear, the medicated water must be taken away from the pigeons immediately. They must be provided with plain, fresh water, into which we can mix drugs that protect the liver (e.g. choline). Grape sugar (glucose) and B vitamins also have beneficial effects.

Note

We must be particularly careful when performing the next treatment with dimetridazole, as pigeons who have survived the poisoning become highly sensitive to it!

*

Unfortunately overdoses of **antibiotics** are a very common phenomenon. Even if administered in the correct dose, an antibiotic has a certain amount of harmful side-effects, but we can accept these because the beneficial effect is greater, and thus on balance the treatment has positive results. If we overdose the medicine, however, the beneficial effect is not increased, while the adverse side-effects grow exponentially, such that they can even outstrip the useful ones. The final result of the treatment is thus a negative one – that is, rather than getting better, the pigeon becomes more ill.

As substances that are **foreign to the body**, **antibiotics** can **attack the pigeon's system at a number of different points.** They represent a direct burden on the liver, which is responsible for detoxification, and put a burden on the systems responsible for excretion (kidneys, intestines, skin). They cause indirect damage by destroying the normal intestinal bacteria – this has a negative effect on the body for a number of reasons. Firstly, **harmful residents of the intestines** are given more room for manoeuvre; secondly, **digestion** and thereby the effectiveness of absorption declines, and toxic substances are absorbed from the gut; thirdly, the **vitamin-producing** role (B vitamins, vitamin K) played by beneficial intestinal residents disappears. After all this it is no surprise if a pigeon, already weakened by the illness, cannot survive the treatment. We could equally say that a badly-selected antibiotic, or one that is well-selected but overdosed, is the last nail in the bird's coffin. (An antibiotic that is selected "blind" and happens to be an unfortunate choice with no effect on the pathogen is an outright overdose from the start, as it brings no beneficial results which might compensate the damaging side-effects of the antibiotic.)

Allergy to antibiotics exists amongst pigeons, even if this is not public knowledge. If one particular pigeon is sensitive to a given agent, it can become seriously ill even if the dose administered is correct, and may die immediately. In fact a fraction of the prescribed dose is enough to induce this. Allergy to antibiotics (which is probably becoming increasingly widespread) must be responsible for many as yet unexplained deaths.

Other poisonings

Rat killer poisoning

If pigeons somehow come into contact with rat or mouse killer containing dicumarol, poisoning can result. The poison inhibits blood coagulation, causing the death of the poisoned bird, which takes place a relatively long time, some days, after the poison is consumed.

Even in natural circumstances capillary ruptures occur in animals' bodies on a continuous basis, and these generally heal immediately. Dicumarol restricts blood coagulation, however, and poisoned birds slowly but surely bleed to death from wounds that are often invisible to the naked eye.

If the capillary rupture takes place near some body openings or in the intestinal wall, fresh blood that cannot coagulate seeps out of the opening into the outside world. However, the bleeding often occurs internally, inside cavities, leaving no external blood marks; without an autopsy the cause often remains a mystery.

Within a few days, the poisoned bird becomes short of blood: the conjunctiva and the mucous membrane of the buccal cavity turn as white as snow. The bird is increasingly dispirited, then becomes distinctly lethargic, and in the absence of treatment it will slowly bleed to death over the space of a few days.

Poisoning with rat killer is easy to treat, its special and efficient **antidote being vitamin K**. The poison acts in the system by competitively inhibiting vitamin K, and as the presence of vitamin K is necessary for normal blood coagulation, its absence leads to haemophilia, the incapacity of the blood to clot. Vitamin K can be administered as an injection and orally; the treatment is easy to perform. Poisoning from rat killer is dangerous because in most cases it is not discovered, as initially the poisoned bird is entirely free of symptoms, and often it is only in the hours before its death that its lethargic behaviour and weakness become obvious. (This is also true for poisoning of other domestic or farm animals with dicumarol.) As many days pass from the intake of the poison to the development of the symptoms, cases of death from rat poison are often not associated with its intake.

Note

Even a very small amount of dicumarol can be deadly. Many a cat or dog has died after eating a poisoned mouse or rat. On such occasions they are killed by the poison consumed by the rat while still alive, which is not a large quantity. As the poison is administered in granulated form or "stuck" onto coloured grains, the consumption of one or two such grains of feed can represent a deadly dose for a pigeon.

Fungal toxins

Fungal toxins are produced by the mould fungi that spread in feed that is incorrectly stored (in a warm and damp place). We discussed this in detail in the section "Fungi-induced diseases".

Insecticides

In the course of treatment against external parasites, we should take care to use products that are certain to be harmless to pigeons! A few active ingredients are harmless for some domestic mammals, but can be severely or fatally poisonous for birds, even if applied externally. One example is diazinon, the "proper" external application of which has repeatedly caused the mass death of pigeon flocks. Most organic phosphoric acid-acetate derivatives (agents in plant-protecting insecticides) are also dangerous, as they can also be **absorbed through the skin**, causing a quick death.

Plant poisons

Many fanciers have described how, a few hours after releasing pigeons – even if only into the courtyard – inexplicable diseases have suddenly appeared, often causing death. On occasions like this, it is probable that the victim has pecked at some part of a plant growing "in the wild" (maybe a mushroom) which contained poison. The identification of this poison is usually an impossible task, but we should suspect plant poisoning if the symptoms appear soon after the pigeons are released, particularly if this occurs repeatedly and we find no other explanation for the problem.

Furthermore, with changes to climate (global warming), new, previously unknown plant types are settling in certain areas, including some that contain poisons. Indeed, long-term changes to the weather will mean that the metabolism of traditional plants in some areas might also change, and transform from weak poisons to more severe ones. Thus, particularly in countries with milder climates, we can – as in the case of arthropods – expect some poisonous types of plant to proliferate better than previously.

Corrosive substances

It is usually as a result of human carelessness or negligence that corrosive materials (alkalis, formalin, acids, undiluted blue vitriol, etc.) find themselves on the surface of pigeons, or more rarely within their bodies.

In cases of **external contamination** we should immediately wash the affected parts of the pigeon's body with ample amounts of water, of course taking great care of our own skin (and eyes)! Afterwards, if we have freed the birds of most of the poison, we can continue the treatment, repeatedly washing the dirtied parts of the body with ample amounts of solution that is slightly acidic (sparkling mineral water, water with vinegar) in the case of alkaline contamination, or slightly alkaline (bicarbonate of soda) in the case of acidic contamination.

In cases of **internal contamination** we should supply birds with plain water and gentle acid or alkali, whichever is in opposition to the poison, as above. After performing this first aid, we should immediately ask for the advice of a veterinarian!

Note

It is common practice to make a bird drink milk after being poisoned. This can be beneficial in a few cases (certain corrosive substances), but if the poisoning is caused by an organic material, for instance, it is downright destructive! Organic substances are generally fat-soluble, and so are capable of being absorbed from the gut in even greater quantities when dissolved in milk fat. With poisonings of this type we should – until a veterinarian gives specialist treatment – provide adsorbent substances, i.e. medical carbon or zeolite, as well as a water-soluble laxative, like Epsom salt, or a non-absorbed oil-based laxative like paraffin oil.

IV. Products grouped by active ingredients

Even a simple listing of the medicines, healing products and nutritional supplements that can be administered to pigeons is beyond the scope of this book, and what is more, these can be acquired under different brand names in different countries. It is much easier to list the active ingredients only, as there are many fewer of these, and they can be discussed in a universal way around the world.

If we are aware of the agent we are looking for, a veterinarian or pharmacist can help us choose between the products that are available locally. Put the other way around, if we read the active ingredient on the packaging of a medicine, we can be clear about its expected effects, side-effects, and the possibility of combining it with other products. (In contrast, the brand name of a product does not generally tell us very much.)

We have grouped the active ingredients according as follows:

1. Antibiotics, chemotherapy drugs
2. Other antibacterial agents, probiotics
3. Drugs affecting the metabolism
   3.a Immune boosters
   3.b Performance boosters
4. Antiparasitic drugs
5. Antifungal drugs
6. Vaccines
7. Disinfectants

*

"Off label" use of medicines

Not all of the agents listed in the book, particularly antibiotics, can be acquired as products approved for pigeons. We find these agents in medicines produced for other species of animal, principally poultry. This counts as off label use, which is possible and often necessary, though the dosage may be different for pigeons that what we find in the medicine's instructions (e.g. for broiler chickens). For this reason, in this section we list the therapeutic dosage for pigeons in terms of the **pure active ingredient** (if this is necessary). From this we can always calculate the required amount of the product as we have it at our disposal, even if the description of the medicine contains no dosage for pigeons.

Let us take an example! Typically doxycycline is the antibiotic that we use regularly and with good results, but which is not often listed among products approved for administering to pigeons. When discussing it we note that **the dose of pure (100%) active ingredient is 0.1g per litre** of drinking water. From this we can calculate the real amount for the product containing doxycycline that we have at our disposal.

For this, we first have to know the percentage of the agent in the product – in everyday terms, the product's concentration. This is usually given in the name of the medicine, and if not, can easily be calculated from the information marked on the packaging. If we know this, we can use the following simple equation to calculate the required amount of the product:

The required amount of the product is equal to the dose of the pure active ingredient divided by the concentration of the product expressed as a percentage, multiplied by a hundred.

required amount of the product =

dose of pure ingredient / concentration of product as % x 100

The dose of active ingredient for doxycycline **is 0.1g per litre of drinking water.** If, for example, the doxycycline product we have is powder of **10% concentration**, the required amount of this product is:

0.1 (g/litre) / **10%** x 100 = 1 (g/litre)

That is to say, 1g of 10% concentration product is needed in each litre of water.

Let us look at another example, in this case for body weight! The dosage of active ingredient for norfloxacin is **0.02g per kilogram of body weight**. The product at our disposal happens to be a **20%** norfloxacin solution.

Required amount of this product is:

0.02 (g/kg body weight) / **20%** x 100 = 0.1 (g/kg of body weight)

As in this example we are dealing with liquid medication (1 gram of which approximately equals 1 ml), we use 0.1 ml of 20% norfloxacin solution for every kg of body weight.

* * *

Important!

If we give medicine to meat **pigeons condemned for human consumption**, we should always find out about the product's withdrawal period for pigeons, and strictly keep to it! The majority of the agents listed in this book cannot be given to birds bred for their meat, or only under strict conditions, and so such pigeons should only be given medicines or therapeutic products as ordered and instructed by a veterinarian.

The withdrawal period is given in terms of days, and this means that at least that many whole days must pass between the last day of treatment and the **slaughter** of the meat pigeon. (Not between the last day of treatment and the bird's **consumption**! Days spent in the refrigerator or the freezer do not count as part of the withdrawal period!) If the withdrawal period is not observed, consumption of the meat which still contains traces of the medicine can cause illness in those with medicine allergies, which in severe instances can even be fatal.

* * *

1. Antibiotics

Antibiotics are very strong substances (poisons!) for use in the battle against bacteria. They kill bacteria or prevent their proliferation. When discussing them, however, we must start by mentioning the fact that the resistance of bacteria to antibiotics, that is **the ineffectiveness of antibiotics, grows with alarming speed**. This state of affairs is primarily alarming because this observation also holds true for human healthcare – bacterial strains have developed that are resistant to practically all existing antibiotics, and it is not rare for these to cause serious illness or death.

The situation is similar in veterinary science and so in pigeon healthcare: most drugs that were selling like hot cakes only recently now have a limited or occasional effect at best. The cause of this situation – in both human and veterinary healthcare – is **the use of antibiotics** that is unnecessary and/or **that does not observe the basic rules**.

Fortunately, the continuous research of pharmaceutical companies generates newer and newer active ingredients for use in treatment, but this does not exonerate us from the rules of administering antibiotics. In most countries, antibiotics for the treatment of animals can only be used as ordered or prescribed by a licensed veterinarian. But whether the breeder, in our case the pigeon fancier, really complies with the rules concerning the use of antibiotics in his yard principally depends on him. We will soon see that it is in everyone's own interests to do so.

The dosage of antibiotics should always be determined for the flock and for each illness, and here we repeat in no uncertain terms that **THE PRE-REQUISITE FOR EFFICIENT AND ECONOMICAL TREATMENT IS AN ACCURATE DIAGNOSIS**. In this case, an accurate diagnosis should include the established sensitivity to antibiotics of the bacterium strain in question!

In addition, the rules that must be observed during treatment with antibiotics are as follows:

- the antibiotics **must not be used in partial doses**, that is in doses smaller than that prescribed
- they must be administered for **at least three consecutive days**

If we give a small dose, or interrupt the course prematurely, **the bacterial strain, weakened or attenuated but not entirely destroyed, revives**; what is more, **it can acquire protection (resistance)** against one or a number of antibiotics at the same time, and thus resists later treatment even if it is administered properly.

The time period of antibiotic treatment varies, usually from three to five days. **In the case of paratyphoid**, a longer period of treatment is advised, lasting **eight to ten or even fourteen days**! Ornithosis requires even longer, possibly a continual course of as much as a month(!), in the light of the veterinarian's tests and prescription.

Following treatment with antibiotics, for 4-5 days we should administer probiotics, that is a product containing live intestinal bacteria! The antibiotic usually destroys the normal intestinal bacteria as well, and so the equilibrium of the pigeon's intestinal flora is upset, which can cause digestive disorders, and in the longer term lead to deficiency illnesses.

*

Even the most carefully selected and expertly administered antibiotics have **side-effects** of varying intensity. If usage **is unnecessary, or not targeted, and therefore does not "hit the spot", or if it is in too large a quantity**, these side-effects can be even more significant. Although antibiotics provided on a routine basis with guesswork **might** bring successful results, this is normally only **random and temporary**. It may repel some of the harmful bacteria, as a result of which the pigeon does indeed temporarily have more energy for other objectives (e.g. racing), but at the same time can also cause damage to the bird's body which is of longer-term effect. It destroys the normal intestinal bacteria, the result of which will be inadequate digestion and bad absorption, which can bring with it intestinal inflammation, hepatic dystrophy and a shortage of vitamins, trace elements or even macro elements. The antibiotic itself can be damaging for some internal organs, especially the liver. Carbohydrate-metabolic disorder can be the consequence of this, and so the muscles performing the work do not receive enough nutrients during flight. In the long term we will certainly not get top performance from a body bleeding from numerous wounds like this.

Many breeders use antibiotics even when this is unnecessary or even harmful. Using antibiotics in the case of fungal infection is a severe mistake, for example, as it has no effect on the fungi, but disrupts the balance between bacteria and fungi in the body by repelling good bacteria, leaving the going clear for fungi, which can cause illness and death if they overproliferate. If someone mistakes a fungal infection for a bacterial one, and treats it accordingly (wrong diagnosis), he should prepare for the worst. I should add that even professionals are often not capable of establishing a correct diagnosis without exhaustive tests, and so attention must again be drawn to targeted treatment, which is based on the fast, relatively cheap, and certainly economical method of culturing bacteria (or fungi).

With a bacterial illness like paratyphoid, an antibiotic chosen blind and therefore possibly incorrectly can be doubly damaging to the system. Rather than get better, a pigeon suffering from salmonellas will find itself in an even worse state as a result of treatment with antibiotics.

What happens on such occasions? The randomly chosen drug has no effect on the salmonella, which happens to be resistant, while it has every effect on the intestinal bacteria, destroying it within hours. The result: the medicine leaves the salmonella unaffected, while **the protection provided by the normal intestinal bacteria also disappears**, and so **the pathogen present in the intestine can proliferate further without hindrance**. (We discuss the protection of intestinal bacteria in more detail in the next section.)

This is the latest example of how we can cause more harm than good with treatment. A typical case is when a highly-respected breeder tells us, maybe from a distance of many hundreds of miles by telephone or e-mail, what we should treat our pigeons with, because it worked well for him. Maybe he is fortunate and happens upon the right thing, but let us think about it: what is the chance that a distant flock contains the same strains of bacteria as our own one?

We should also use antibiotics with care because many of them not only have a negative effect on the birds' performance, but also a detrimental effect on the reproductive cycle, including pairing just as much as the propensity to lay eggs and raise chicks, something that has often given fanciers headaches. It is particularly more prolonged antibiotic treatment that can have such, very disadvantageous side-effects. For this reason, the targeted form of treatment is advised, particularly in the breeding season; indeed, if the period of treatment is longer than five days, it is worth culturing bacteria again while it is still in progress, as this can provide important indications as to how it should be continued or altered.

It can happen, of course, that it becomes necessary to administer an antibiotic that is harmful to reproduction in the breeding season or to performance in the racing season. We have to weigh up which is the lesser problem: omitting the treatment, or the treatment's side-effects. This always has to be decided in the given situation, and no general advice can be given. (But there is one piece of practical advice: if a bacterial inflammation is still limited to the intestinal system, then it is advisable to administer an antibiotic orally that is not absorbed from the gut – in this way, it has a good local effect, but the least damaging side-effects on the other organs. It is even more fortunate if one of the antibiotics under consideration causes less damage – according to culturing – to beneficial intestinal bacteria.)

In the course of our discussion of antibiotics, let us not forget that **antibiotics in and of themselves do not cure the ill bird!** Antibiotics are just one type of assistance for the system – one that is encumbered with side-effects. The **illness itself is defeated by the immune system** – if this does not work efficiently, even the best and most expensive antibiotic treatment is doomed to failure.

Certain antibiotics have a distinct immunosuppressive effect, but in general we can say of all of them that they inhibit the immune system indirectly – if administered on a regular basis, they make the body sterile, allowing the immune system to "become lazy".

* * *

We will discuss the individual antibiotics according to the following considerations:

Grouping into families, spectrum of effect
Practical characteristics, absorption, toxicity
Drug interactions
Contraindications
Dosage

Notes

For practical reasons, we include in the section on antibiotics other drugs which have a similar indication (e.g. sulfonamides).

It is worth knowing which antibiotics belong to which family (e.g. penicillins, quinolones, macrolides, sulfonamides, etc.), because if a given bacterial strain is resistant to a certain antibiotic, it is probable that it will be resistant to all other members of that family.

Dosage calculated relative to drinking water (gram of active ingredient per litre of water) takes the average daily consumption of water into account. On hot days, or if an above average level of water is consumed for other reasons, we should only take this average amount of water consumption as our reference point, and always use it to calculate the daily dosage of the medicine!

To achieve and maintain the effective level of antibiotics in the bloodstream as quickly as possible, it can, thanks to their absorption and release characteristics, and unless the veterinarian prescribes otherwise, be advisable to give one and a half or two times the dose on the first occasion.

* * *

amoxicillin

Penicillin derivative with a broad spectrum. Very effective against salmonella, coli, cocci and haemophilus, but has no effect on mycoplasma and chlamydia.

Is absorbed quickly and well from the gut, to an extent of about 80%, and so it can equally be administered when intestinal inflammation occurs or when other organs are bacterially infected, all the more so because its absorption is hardly influenced by the quantity of the intestinal contents. It is less toxic, and can be given in breeding and racing seasons. As its release from the system is also fast, the daily dosage should be divided into two parts or added to drinking water continuously.

Its disadvantage is that certain bacterial strains (some salmonella, coli and coccus strains) produce a substance called beta lactamase, with which they decompose the amoxicillin, making it ineffective against them. (See the following paragraph!)

Drug interactions: Given together with aminoglicosides, the two enhance one another's effect. Combination with gentamycin gives a very broad spectrum of antibacterial effect.

Dosage: 0.15-0.2 grams per litre of drinking water, or 0.015-0.02 grams per kilo of body weight, over 4-5 days (10-14 days in the case of salmonellosis). In severe cases or those of respiratory illness we use the higher dose.

amoxicillin + clavulanic acid

The aforementioned salmonella, coli and coccus strains are not capable of breaking down amoxicillin with clavulanic acid, and so this combination is effective against them. As the cost of the combination is many times more than that of simple amoxicillin, it is best only to use it when needed, and following a susceptibility test.

The combination is quickly absorbed from the intestine, and its absorption is not affected by the intestinal contents.

Clavulanic acid is highly sensitive to moisture, and can easily be ruined even by humidity in the air. For this reason, it should be stored in packaging that can be closed airtight, while using hygroscopic material!

Dosage: 0.15-0.2 grams per litre of drinking water, or 0.015-0.02 grams per kilo of body weight, over 4-5 days (10-14 days in the case of salmonellosis). In severe cases or cases of respiratory illness we use the higher dose.

ampicillin

Penicillin derivative with a broad spectrum, primarily effective against coli and salmonella bacteria. Many have reported that resistance spreads quickly, and so we should use in a targeted fashion if possible! It has no effect on mycoplasma and chlamydia.

Administered orally, part of it is quickly absorbed, but the quantity of intestinal content influences its absorption, and so it should always be given on an empty stomach. It is released from the body quickly, so its daily dosage should be divided into two or three parts, or provided on a continuous basis. The system withstands it well, as it is less toxic for organs. Our experience shows that the bacterium strains of normal intestinal flora are increasingly resistant to it.

Contraindication: Should not be given to birds less than two weeks old!

Dosage: 1 gram per litre of drinking water, or 0.1 grams per kilo of body weight, over 5 days. (10 days in the event of salmonellosis.)

apramycin

Antibiotic with a relatively broad spectrum that belongs to the aminoglicosides. It is effective against coli and especially against salmonella, all the more so because resistance has not really developed to it. It is also effective against cocci and certain species of mycoplasma.

It is only absorbed moderately or poorly from the gut, and so if administered orally is only really effective against processes limited to the intestines. It is moderately toxic for the system, and prolonged dosage can cause renal dystrophy.

Contraindication: Must not be administered in the event of renal dysfunction (e.g. from PMV infection)!

Drug interactions: Can be combined with penicillin derivatives or cephalosporins.

Dosage: 0.4-0.5 grams per litre of drinking water, or 0.04-0.05 grams per kilo of body weight, over 5 days (10 days in the case of salmonellosis).

cephalosporin

Semi-synthetic penicillin derivative. Is also well absorbed if administered orally. Its spectrum of effect is narrow – it is primarily effective against cocci. It has a limited effect on salmonella and coli strains. It has no effect on mycoplasma and chlamydia. It is principally recommended for respiratory diseases caused by cocci, and for purulent skin inflammations.

It is not toxic, and has no significant side-effects on the body. If put in water, the pigeons are happy to drink it.

Contraindication: Must not be administered in the event of renal dysfunction that involves reduced or increased urine production.

Drug interactions: Can be given together with apramycin.

Dosage: 0.3 grams per litre of drinking water, or 0.03 grams per kilo of body weight, over 6 days.

chlortetracycline

A tetracycline with a broad spectrum of antibacterial effect. It is particularly effective against mycoplasma and chlamydia, as well as against most bacteria causing respiratory disease. Although in principle it is also effective against coli and salmonellas, unfortunately in practice these pathogens are often resistant to it, and so we should only administer it for these on a targeted basis. (Though we should note that everyday experience suggests the resistance against it is less than in the case of oxytetracycline.)

We always administer chlortetracycline on an empty stomach, in water acidified with apple vinegar. In the course of its use, supplements containing lime must not be given, as the calcium in the lime neutralizes it and renders it useless. It is also damaged by iron, magnesium and zinc (non-enamelled metal dishes). When using chlortetracycline it is advisable to boil the drinking water beforehand if water is very hard in our area (if detergent does not froth easily)! The hardness of the water is caused by the large quantities of calcium and magnesium in it, most of which we can get rid of by simply boiling the water.

When administering chlortetracycline we should also avoid products containing electrolytes.

It is more toxic for the body and more harmful to normal intestinal bacteria than doxycycline.

When given to young birds, however, it gives less rise for worry than does doxycycline.

Drug interactions: If necessary, it can very successfully be combined with tylosin or with tiamulin.

Contraindication: Chlortetracycline cannot be used in the event of existing renal dysfunction (increased urine production because of disease caused by paramyxovirus, or the opposite, reduced urine production due to kidney deficiency).

Dosage: 1 gram per litre of drinking water, or 0.1 grams per kilo of body weight, for 3-5 days (many weeks in the case of ornithosis).

colistin

Colistin (or polymyxin E) is very effective against salmonella and coli. Compared to other antibiotics, resistance to it occurs more rarely.

It is hardly absorbed from the gut at all, and so if given orally its effect is limited to the intestinal canal. If administered in injection form, it is absorbed quickly and completely, but it is a **strongly toxic** compound for kidneys, and so should only be injected if this is justified, and on the basis of a preliminary susceptibility test.

Drug interactions: Colistin can be combined with enrofloxacin, this combination is very effective against salmonellas.

It must not be given at the same time as other antibiotics, medicines or vitamins, or immediately afterwards.

Contraindication: Because of its strong toxicity, it is not advisable to give it in breeding season or to young birds.

Dosage: 0.1 grams per litre of drinking water, or 0.01 grams per kilo of body weight, for 3, perhaps 4-5 days.

difloxacin

Fourth-generation quinolone derivative with a **very broad spectrum of antibacterial effect**. Has an effect on salmonella, coli, mycoplasma, cocci, haemophilus, chlamydia. Its area of indication is similar to that of the third-generation enrofloxacin: it can also be used for intestinal inflammation, respiratory diseases, cystitis and inflammations of the reproductive organs, inflammation of the joints and skin infections.

As it is a new agent, we have relatively little information about it at our disposal. But our own experience suggests that resistance to it develops more quickly than in the case of enrofloxacin.

It is easily absorbed from the intestine and so is effective if used orally. Its release from the system is relatively quick, and so we add it to drinking water on a continuous basis, i.e. during the period of treatment the pigeons only receive medicated water.

Drug interactions: Given its broad spectrum of effect, this is not advised.

Contraindication: Unknown at present – not enough data is available relating to its use with pigeons. But as it is a quinolone derivative, like enrofloxacin it may cause developmental disorders if given during breeding season or the period of rearing, and so there must be good justification for it being administered at such times.

Dosage: 0.1 grams per litre of drinking water, or 0.01 grams per kilo of body weight, over a space of 3-5 days.

doxycycline

A tetracycline with a broad spectrum. It is particularly effective against mycoplasmas and chlamydias, and against most bacteria responsible for respiratory diseases. Although originally it had a good effect on coli and salmonellas, unfortunately these pathogens are mostly resistant by now, and so doxycycline should only be used against them on the basis of a susceptibility test.

If possible, we should administer it before feeding the birds, in water acidified with apple vinegar, because it is much better absorbed in an acidic environment. Supplements containing lime must not be given during its use, as the calcium in the lime neutralizes the doxycycline – though to a lesser extent than other tetracyclines. Similarly, iron, magnesium and zinc can damage the active ingredient (ferrous water, unenamelled metal pots). Products containing electrolytes should also be avoided when administering it.

When using it, kick-therapy is advised. We give the pigeon the dosage of medicine prescribed for the average amount of water consumed a day or relative to body weight, and make the pigeons drink it at once in a small amount of water, then repeat this every 24 hours.

Unlike other tetracyclines, doxycycline can also be used in the event of renal dysfunction (e.g. illness caused by paramyxovirus). Another advantage is that it is less toxic to the body and damages normal intestinal bacteria less than other tetracyclines do.

Drug interactions: Can effectively be combined with tylosin.

Contraindication: Should not be given to birds less than three weeks old.

Dosage: 0.1 grams per litre of drinking water, or 0.01 grams per kilo of body weight, over a space of 3-5 days. In more severe cases the treatment is recommended for 8-10 days. Ornithosis can even necessitate a cure of 4-5 weeks.

enrofloxacin

Third-generation quinolone derivative with an extremely broad spectrum. Useful against salmonellas, haemophilus, chlamydia, coli, cocci and mycoplasmas. It can equally be used for intestinal inflammation, respiratory illnesses, genito-urinary inflammation, inflammation of the joints and skin infections. Resistance only develops with difficulty, but **its progress is helped by doses smaller than that prescribed!**

It is absorbed well from the intestine, soon reaches the efficient level in the bloodstream, and maintains this for a long time, and so it can also be administered in kick-therapy form, that is giving the entire daily dosage at one time, once a day. It is also very good at penetrating tissues outside the blood system (e.g. skin, body cavities, abscesses). It is less toxic, and the system tolerates it well.

According to many it is currently the most effective antibiotic against paratyphoid in pigeon-breeding. Administering it for 10-14 days can often even eradicate symptom-free infection and the carrying of salmonella. A further advantage of enrofloxacin is that it is not used in human healthcare.

Drug interactions: Administering it in combination with other drugs is not recommended. For one thing, the broad spectrum and the infrequency of resistance make it unnecessary; furthermore, if combined with most other antibiotics, effectiveness decreases.

Contraindication: It is not advisable to administer it in the period of rearing, or only if absolutely necessary. (It can cause problems with chondrification.) In breeding season it can raise the number of infertile eggs if administered directly before or after pairing, when the egg is being formed. Its after-effects can also appear in youngsters, which can manifest itself in insufficient or abnormal development in the first weeks of life.

Dosage: 0.1 grams per litre of drinking water, or 0.01 grams per kilo of body weight, over 3-5 days. A period of 8-10 days is advised in the case of salmonellosis.

erythromycin

An antibiotic belonging to the macrolides, primarily useful for respiratory diseases, which has a good effect on various cocci. It is also effective against haemophilus and mycoplasma. Chlamydias are less responsive to it, however.

It is absorbed quickly and well from the gut, but it must be given before the bird is fed. It is hardly toxic for organs. When administering it we must provide it in drinking water on a continuous basis, taking care that it does not stand in the water for too long, as it has a propensity to break up.

If it absolutely necessary to perform a course of treatment during the period of rearing, its low toxicity can make erythromycin the suitable choice.

Dosage: 0.2 grams per litre of drinking water, or 0.02 grams per kilo of body weight, over 5 days.

furazolidone

An antibacterial drug that has long been in use. Like some sulfonamides, it is enjoying a revival. For pigeons, it can primarily be used against salmonellosis. It is more likely to be effective in those regions in which for some reason it was not used in the past years or decades.

Dosage: 0.25 grams per litre of drinking water, or 0.025 grams per kilo of body weight, over 4-5 days.

gentamycin

One of the most effective of the aminoglicoside derivatives. Its antibacterial spectrum is relatively broad: it is effective against salmonella, coli and cocci. Compared to other antibiotics, resistance to it occurs more rarely.

It is hardly absorbed from the gut at all, and so if given orally its effect is limited to the intestinal canal. If administered in injection form, it is absorbed quickly and completely, but it is a strongly toxic compound, and so should only be injected if this is justified, and on the basis of a preliminary susceptibility test.

Drug interactions: Gentamycin can be combined with amoxicillin (possibly lincomycin), but these are the exceptions. It must not be given at the same time as other antibiotics, medicines or vitamins, or immediately afterwards.

Contraindication: Because of its strong toxicity, it is not advisable to give it in injection form in breeding season or to young birds. Neither can it be administered as an injection in the event of kidney deficiency.

Dosage: 0.5 grams per litre of drinking water, or 0.05 grams per kilo of body weight.

lincomycin

An antibiotic belonging to the lincosamides, related to the macrolides. It is generally effective against bacteria causing respiratory diseases, and thus against mycoplasmas and also cocci. It has no effect on salmonellas and coli. In smaller doses it is bacteriostatic; in larger doses it has a bactericidal effect. Resistance to it only develops slowly.

Only about 20-30% of it is absorbed from the intestines, and intestinal content further limits this absorption, so we should administer it before feeding! If it spends too much time in the (full) crop, it is decomposed by the crop's microflora. So its application in drinking water should always take place on an empty stomach!

If it is not the intestinal system that is the target, its effect is more certain if given in injection form, because of its absorption characteristics. If we give it orally nevertheless, the dose must be doubled.

It is not a toxic antibiotic, and it does not put too great a burden on the system, and so many pigeon flyers use it for (preventive) treatment between races. It still has to be given continuously over three consecutive days, because courses of just a day or two only hasten the development of resistance.

Drug interactions: It can be excellently combined with spectinomycin: the two complement each other's therapeutic spectrum well.

Dosage: 0.15-0.2 (or 0.3-0.4) grams per litre of drinking water if given orally, or 0.015-0.02 grams per kilogram of body weight as an injection, for a minimum of 5 and a maximum of 10 days. (Only 3-5 days if combined with spectinomycin.)

norfloxacin

A third-generation quinolone derivative similar in structure and effect to enrofloxacin. Its therapeutic spectrum extends to include salmonellas, coli, mycoplasma, cocci and haemophilus. It is very effective for intestinal inflammation, respiratory diseases, inflammation of the joints, skin inflammation with abscess formation, and particularly against genito-urinary infections.

Its absorption from the gut is easy and fast, it soon reaches the level of the bloodstream and maintains it for a long time, and so, as in the case of enrofloxacin, we can use it in **kick-therapy** form, administering the daily dose at once (every 24 hours), perhaps divided into two parts. It is less toxic as far as the body is concerned.

Our own experience shows that it is highly effective against salmonellas. In the case of paratyphoid, its effect is about the same as that of enrofloxacin, indeed on some occasions it has proven to be even more effective. For salmonella infections, we should use it for 8-14 days!

Drug interactions: Administering it in combination with other drugs is not recommended.

Contraindication: A course of treatment during the breeding season must be considered just as in the case of enrofloxacin, for it can have a negative effect on the fertility of the eggs.

Dosage: 0.2 grams per litre of drinking water, or 0.02 grams per kilo of body weight, for 3-5 days (8-10 days or as many as 14 days in the case of salmonellosis).

oxytetracycline

A tetracycline with a broad spectrum. Effective against mycoplasmas and chlamydias, and against the majority of the bacteria responsible for respiratory diseases. Although originally it also had a good effect on coli and salmonellas, sadly these pathogens are mostly resistant to it nowadays, and so it can only be used against them as a targeted treatment.

Like chlortetracycline, oxytetracycline should always be given on an empty stomach, in water soured with apple vinegar. During treatment all supplements containing lime must be withdrawn, as the calcium in the lime neutralizes the agent and renders it useless. Iron, magnesium and zinc damage the active ingredient in the same way (unenamelled metal trays). We should also avoid products containing electrolytes when administering it. Preliminary boiling of the water is recommended.

It is more toxic to the body and damaging to normal intestinal bacteria than doxycycline, but despite this its use on young birds gives less cause for concern.

Drug interactions: If necessary, it can successfully be combined with tylosin or tiamulin.

Contraindication: It cannot be used in the event of existing renal deficiency.

Dosage: 0.4-0.5 grams per litre of drinking water, or 0.04-0.05 grams per kilo of body weight, for 3-5 days (many weeks in the case of ornithosis).

spectinomycin

A compound closely related to the aminoglicosides. It is effective against salmonellas and coli, and it also useful against mycoplasmas.

It is not absorbed from the gut. Its absorption is good if given as an injection, but it is also released quickly. It is the least toxic of the aminoglicosides. It is less of a burden on the system, and so it can also be used in racing season.

As spectinomycin is not absorbed from the intestine, if administered orally it can be used for enteritis during the breeding season without risk.

Drug interactions: It is very good in combination with lincomycin, and this is the form in which it is generally distributed. On its own we are more likely to find it as an injection.

Dosage: 0.2 grams per litre of drinking water, or 0.02 grams per kilo of body weight, for 3, perhaps 4-5 days.

streptomycin

An aminoglicoside. A bactericide, it is effective on salmonella, coli and haemophilus strains, as well as certain cocci.

It is not absorbed from the intestine. Given as an injection it is quickly absorbed, but also quickly released, and so it is advisable to use it twice a day.

It is a toxic compound which is released through the kidneys and bile. It puts a burden on the liver, and has a very harmful effect on the kidneys and the ears.

Our experience shows that normal intestinal bacteria are increasingly resistant to it.

Drug interactions: It is effective in combination with penicillin. Must not be administered at the same time as tetracyclines or sulfonamides.

Contraindication: Should not be given at a young age, particularly not in injection form. Neither can it be used in the event of insufficient functioning of the liver or existing kidney problems.

Dosage: 0.4-0.5 grams per litre of drinking water, or 0.04-0.05 grams per kilo of body weight, for 3-4 or at most 5 days.

sulfachlorpyridazine

A compound belonging to the sulfonamides, which is generally used in combination with trimethoprim (potentiated sulfonamide). It is effective against salmonella, coli and haemophilus strains, and also has a good effect on mycoplasmas.

Is absorbed well from the gut, but its release is also quick, which must be taken into account when administering it (continuous provision in drinking water). Its toxicity is low, but it must not be given in the event of insufficient functioning of the kidneys!

Sulfonamides are antibacterial agents that have long been in use (since the 1940s), and so a broad resistance has developed to them. Thanks to this widespread resistance and prevalence of modern antibiotics, their use has declined in recent decades. But precisely for this reason, nowadays some sulfonamides are again showing a high level of effectiveness.

Contraindication: Should only be administered with care in the event of low consumption of water, e.g. because of illnesses caused by haemophilus.

Dosage: 0.15-0.24 grams per litre of drinking water, or 0.015-0.024 grams per kilo of body weight, for at least 3-5 days (10-14 days in the case of salmonellosis).

tiamulin

A semi-synthetic pleuromutilin derivative. It is very effective against **mycoplasmas**, and also has an effect on most staphylococcus and streptococcus strains. It has no effect on salmonella and coli, however.

It is absorbed very quickly and well from the gut, and so it reaches the therapeutic level in the bloodstream within 2-3 hours of being administered orally.

Drug interactions: Can be combined well with tetracyclines.

Dosage: 0.25 grams per litre of drinking water, or 0.025 grams per kilo of body weight.

tilozin

A macrolide with a relatively broad spectrum. It is very effective against the cocci and mycoplasmas that cause respiratory diseases (more so than erythromycin, also a macrolide), although certain mycoplasma strains are already resistant to it. It has no effect on salmonella and coli.

It is absorbed well from the gut, but its release from the body is also fast. It can reach a high level of concentration in the lungs and the joints. It is not toxic, and is tolerated well by the system, but in the event of heavy strain it can cause a decline in performance.

To prevent the spread of mycoplasma it can also be used for the disinfecting soaking of breeding eggs, with a concentration of 2.5g per litre.

In combination, it is very effective in the event of complications.

Drug interactions: Can very successfully be combined with tetracyclines and with certain sulfonamides (e.g. sulfachlorpyrazine). Combining it with tetracyclines leads to a stronger effect against mycoplasma, while administering it together with sulfonamides broadens the spectrum of effect: this combination is suitable for repelling cocci, mycoplasmas, haemophilus, coli and salmonellas, even coccidia, all at the same time.

Its effect is decreased by lincomycin, however, and should not be combined with it!

Dosage: 0.5 grams per litre of drinking water, or 0.05 grams per kilo of body weight, over the space of 3-5 days.

You can see ***Table 4. Therapeutic spectrum of antibiotics*** *at the very end of the book.*

2. Other antibacterial agents, probiotics

In addition to antibiotics, there are many other drugs that have an antibacterial effect within the system, i.e. are capable of destroying, attenuating, or otherwise repelling bacteria that have entered the body. They have a number of advantages compared to antibiotics:

- they are generally natural ingredients, and so unwanted side-effects are most often insignificant, and are less of a burden on the body and the environment

- only rarely does resistance to them emerge

- administering them often makes the use of antibiotics unnecessary

- they usually improve the performance of racing pigeons

- some also have antifungal or certain antiviral properties

Their use on their own is primarily recommended for preventive treatment or for overcoming minor infections. In severe cases, they serve well as supplements or follow-ups to antibiotic treatment. Because of these advantages, we should use these drugs instead of antibiotics if at possible.

Antibacterial agents

Immunoglobulins

Ready-to-use antibodies that we give to the body of the ill bird to support the immune system. They exist in different forms (IgG, IgA, IgM), and can be effective against a number of pathogens (viruses, bacteria, parasites). If an infection threatens, they also can be used for preventive treatment.

With pigeons, they can be very useful in the treatment or prevention of viral diseases, all the more so because the repertoire of effective drugs that can be taken is very limited. This is particularly true of infections and diseases caused by adenovirus type I and circovirus.

On average, we should use them for 7 days for treatment and for 3 days for prevention.

Essential oils

They can be used in spray form that can be administered to the throat, or as nose drops. They have bactericidal characteristics, helping to defeat the pathogens which attack the respiratory passages. They also increase the blood flow of the mucous membrane of the respiratory passages, causing local hyperaemia. As a result of all this, they prevent the accumulation of mucus in the respiratory passages, guarantee greater and more efficient exchange of air, which results in an improvement to flying performance.

Their use is particularly recommended before and after races, but they are also helpful "off-season". They provide good supplementary therapy during antibiotic treatments.

Other herbal extracts, teas

Like essential oils, these can help to keep the respiratory passages clean, but we primarily administer them orally, because they have a particularly beneficial effect on the intestinal system. They repel the pathogenic bacteria and parasites hiding in the gut, including coccidia. The blood supply to the digestive tract is increased, making digestion more efficient and easy. This is a big advantage, for if a pigeon uses less of its energies on digestion, it has more energy left for flying.

Another advantage is that they are excellent sources of trace and micro elements, elements which in today's world are not to be found in sufficient quantities in pigeon feed. A further advantage is that herbs are normally grown without chemicals and artificial fertilizer or are collected from their natural habitat, and so in principle they should be free of damaging substances. If at all possible, we should use such organic herbs, or their extracts, from places free of chemicals.

We usually provide them in drinkable form (teas, tinctures), but they can also be administered as nasal drops or sprays. On the other hand, their overuse can be a burden on the system (liver, normal intestinal bacteria), and so they must only be used according to the recommended dose and for the prescribed period.

Probiotics

Probiotics are products that **contain useful intestinal bacteria** (enterococci, lactobacilli) in a form capable of proliferation. Administered orally, these beneficial germs reach the intestinal system and begin to proliferate, rejuvenating or supplementing the normal flora, that have for whatever reason declined.

The useful bacteria in the intestines perform essential tasks for the health of the host system:

- they **assist digestion and utilization of nutrients** by breaking them up with their own enzymes
- they **produce useful substances**, including vitamins B and K

- they **restrain pathogenic bacteria**

The latter function is extremely important and necessary, as it primarily affects **salmonella** and **coli** bacteria.

There are two ways in which intestinal bacteria have their protective effect. Firstly, through their metabolism they produce a slightly **acidic environment** around themselves, which is not favourable for the proliferation of salmonella and coli bacteria. Secondly, simply the quantity of adequately proliferated intestinal bacteria represents a **mechanical barrier** for pathogens – they cover the wall of the intestine and its villi with a number of layers, and so they make it harder for the salmonella and coli bacteria, already attenuated by the acidic environment, to reach or enter the intestinal wall.

A decrease in the number of intestinal bacteria can be the cause of severe illnesses. **Normal intestinal bacteria can be damaged to a high degree as a result of antibiotic treatment**, as most antibiotics are also effective against them. Some antibiotics destroy them completely, making the intestinal contents sterile, which often has more serious consequences than the illness itself for which the medicine was taken. **Inadequate consumption of feed** over many days is also detrimental to intestinal bacteria, as they cannot find the right conditions for life in the insufficient intestinal contents.

It is important that in these instances we **supplement** these useful bacteria **by artificial means**. **After antibiotic treatment** we should always give probiotics for 4-5 days! They are very useful in stress situations, especially if this is combined with the risk of infection (races, transportation). Irrespective of this, we should administer probiotics once or twice a week, thereby continuously refreshing the stock of normal intestinal bacteria.

Note

We can provide nestlings with normal intestinal bacteria from a natural source, just as young birds acquire them in natural circumstances. The chicks receive these bacteria through the parent birds' excrement, and so many fanciers use the technique of exposing the chicks to the natural "infection" earlier than usual, that is they place them on the floor. The method is effective, but **only if the faeces of the pigeons kept in the loft is free of pathogenic bacteria, viruses and parasites**, otherwise we only spread e.g. salmonellas amongst the young birds before their time. It is worth considering how justified this method is today, what with the threat of circovirus. Perhaps it is better if – as in the case of both intensive and extensive poultry production (chickens, geese, etc.) – we supply pigeon chicks with probiotics that are certainly free of pathogens **in the first few days of their lives**.

*

Different products vary in the quality and quantity of the useful intestinal bacteria types they contain. If possible, we should use a product that includes a number of different strains, and in addition it is advisable to alternate between products.

Most products also contain vitamins, and so a separate dosage of vitamins is unnecessary or possibly even detrimental.

We should take particular care when storing probiotics, as too much heat can easily ruin them, as can dampness in the air.

* * *

Important!

As we have repeatedly noted in this book, culturing of bacteria from faeces not only tells us which antibiotics may have an effect on the pathogen that is present, but also which antibiotics will NOT have an effect on the normal (beneficial) intestinal bacteria. If we are lucky, we can find medicine that destroys the pathogen but leaves the benevolent residents of the intestines in peace, and this will speed up the recovery of the ill bird enormously.

Over and above this, as our own experiments and experiences have shown, we can do our bit to help our luck.

The method is easy. When we set off towards the veterinarian with the ill birds or their dropping samples in tow, we should also take the probiotics that we normally use. On the way we should pop into a dairy store and buy a selection of different good quality natural yogurts containing live cultures (e.g. Caucasian yogurt, known as kefir). We then request the veterinarian, in addition to the faeces sample, to spread a little of the probiotic on another culture plate, and a drop of the yogurt on a third.

By the time the pathogen's susceptibility to medicine is revealed, the probiotic and the beneficial bacteria of the yogurt will have proliferated on the other two plates. Comparing the three plates, we will very likely find an antibiotic that has an effect on the pathogen, but which is tolerated by the bacteria of the yogurt or the factory-made probiotic.

If there is such an antibiotic, then – in contrast to the usual method – **we do not have to wait for the end of the antibiotic treatment to give probiotics** (or yogurt). These can be given from the first moment, as the active intestinal flora and thus normal digestion can be maintained throughout the treatment, which is in itself a victory. With this little trick up our sleeve, **the intestinal system of the ill bird can be launched in the direction of recovery within hours**, and often by the following day we will have an entirely healthy pigeon on our hands. There is no need to explain why this is particularly important in the case of young, severely ill, or perhaps racing pigeons…

For purposes of illustration, *Table 5 (at the very end of the book)* presents data based on our own series of tests. Naturally these tests must always be conducted with the given pigeon flock and the natural and artificial probiotics that are available locally, and then be compared to results for the susceptibility of the pathogen.

This method can also be used in the case of respiratory diseases; indeed, it will be even easier for us to find antibiotics that are effective against the pathogen, but which do not harm useful bacteria. The reason for this is that the majority of respiratory diseases are caused by bacteria (e.g. haemophilus, mycoplasma, cocci) that are very different from normal intestinal bacteria. Salmonellas and coli bacteria, which are most commonly responsible for intestinal inflammation, are closely related to normal intestinal bacteria, however, and so the responsiveness of these pathogens to antibiotics is generally more like that of useful bacteria.

Note

We can insert the plain yogurt straight into the crop (with a plastic syringe), but we can also administer it mixed into a little cereal feed. We can add it to drinking water, too, but first we should dilute it in lukewarm water and mix well.

We should not use yogurt when administering tetracycline, because of its high calcium content.

3. Drugs affecting the metabolism

Products affecting the metabolism include vitamins, amino acids, macro and micro elements, trace elements, energy carriers, and, in given proportions, various mixtures of these. We administer them in order to prevent and treat deficiency illnesses, and also for a general strengthening of the system, e.g. as a supplementary treatment in the event of infectious illnesses.

These drugs also have a direct or indirect effect on the immune system, which they support to some extent. We have classified in a separate group those drugs with high immunostimulant capabilities, just as we have done with special substances for increasing racing performance.

*

In this section we are faced with a glut both of products and of active ingredients, as just about all substances that reach the body have an effect on the metabolism. So here we were only able to have a summary classification, primarily based on practical considerations.

*

Amino acids

During the metabolic process, it is protein that has entered the body that produces the least energy relative to its molecular weight, and this is one reason why we usually decrease the protein content of feed, and thereby its amino acid content, before races. (On such occasions we increase the proportion of carbohydrates and fatty acids, which produce more energy relative to their molecular weight.) But during tiring races the musculature has to work very hard, and so has to regenerate very quickly afterwards.

We support this regeneration with products containing amino acids. We should give preference to products that **contain essential amino acids**. These are methionine, lysine, tryptophan, valine, leucine, isoleucine, histidine, phenylalanine, threonine.

Mineral salts, electrolytes

The body's loss of electrolytes is highest in the case of illnesses that cause vomiting and diarrhoea. With these, the overly high amount of water takes much salt out from the system with itself. If we only substitute for the water, the body's salt equilibrium is soon upset.

During lengthy flights the need for electrolytes similarly increases, and so these must quickly be replaced when birds arrive. We should take care with intake of salt **before flights**, however, as the high amount of salt can retain a lot of water in the system, and the pigeon becomes overweight, which worsens its racing performance. For the same reason, we must also be careful when administering vitamins, and **must not under any circumstances exceed the recommended dose before flights**! It is particularly useful if we observe restraint, especially on the day directly before flight.

Herbal teas and extracts

These have a blood-cleansing and anti-poisoning effect. They soothe and regenerate the mucous membrane of the intestinal wall. **They help the development of the young**, and have a positive effect during moulting. **They improve performance**, and speed up regeneration after races. They stimulate the immune system.

It is advisable to administer them in drinking water about twice a week, especially during moulting, or when birds are young. They should be given to racing pigeons one day before caging, then after they arrive.

Hepatoprotective substances

The centre of the metabolic system is the liver. It is an organ with an exceptionally wide variety of functions, which has an unprecedented capacity to regenerate, but a heavy or prolonged burden on it can cause irreversible damage. Its weakened operation can lead to inadequate operation of all the other organs. Liver insufficiency brings disorder in the carbohydrate and fat metabolism, which is tantamount to a decline in flight performance.

There are pathogens which attack the liver directly, e.g. trichomonads, adenovirus type II, or salmonellas. Metal elements are usually also severely damaging to the liver, but most often it is the side-effects of some medicines which cause problems. Dimetridazole and related drugs can be distinctly harmful to the liver, just as are most antibiotics. Most drugs against parasites and fungi can also have a negative effect on the operation of the liver.

When administering such "strong" medicines, it is advisable to accompany them with drugs that protect the liver. We normally find these substances in combined vitamin products.

The following are hepatoprotective substances: methionine, choline, inositol, betaine. Other compounds that protect the liver or support its operation are grape sugar (glucose), vitamin E, and members of the B vitamin group.

Beer yeast

Of great biological value, rich in members of the vitamin B group, and in substances required for protein anabolism. It is particularly beneficial during rearing and recovery, as it helps the body's metabolism in a number of points. We can also use it as a supplementary treatment for illnesses causing neurological symptoms (paramyxovirus, poisonings).

Must be not given during and around courses of antibiotics. It must not be used in the course of treatment with amprolium, nor directly after it.

3.a Immune boosters

dimethylglycine

Dimethylglycine is a drug that has come into use recently, which intercepts the metabolic cycle at a number of points, offering it support.

Because of its distinct immunostimulant effect, it is highly recommended for viral infections (circovirus, adenovirus), as the ammunition at our disposal is anyway limited. It is also perfect as a supplemental therapy for other infectious illnesses, as well as for protecting against stress effects and for stimulating heart activity and circulation. It protects the liver and increases performance.

It is very useful if administered alongside vaccines, as it increases the efficiency of vaccination.

Its dosage is 0.05g per kilogram of body weight, twice a day, administered directly by mouth or mixed in feed. If treatment is prolonged, it needs only to be given once a day from the third week.

trace elements

Amongst other things, trace elements are the essential components of enzymes that play a role in metabolism. They strengthen the immune system, and increase resistance to infections. They boost racing performance, and speed up regeneration after flying.

As the trace element content of the feed is usually unknown to the breeder, and in addition the trace elements in plants are generally on the decline what with the prevalence of artificial fertilizers, it is advisable to give pigeons trace elements on a regular basis, once or twice a week.

A good method of preventing a deficiency of trace elements is if the pigeons' feed is acquired from a number of different locations that are far apart, and feed them with a mixture. This means that possible deficiencies in ingredients are largely corrected.

selenium

A rare element, in 66th place on the list of the most frequent on the Earth. It only appears in small quantities in the body, too, but it is nevertheless essential for life. We discussed it in detail in the section on metabolic illnesses, and here we would like to draw the reader's attention to the fact that it can easily be overdosed, which may lead to poisoning. We should take care not to give a number of different products containing selenium together or directly after one another, or if so, only in small quantities.

zeolite

A mineral of volcanic origins, based on aluminium hydroxy silicate. Its cross-linked crystal structure can hold large quantities of water, which is released by heat, and the material takes on a microporous structure. The spatial structure develops according to the temperature and duration of the heating, and this can be used to make expedient use of the zeolite's adsorbing characteristic. So it becomes suitable for the **selective adsorption of harmful substances**: gases, liquids, even parasitic eggs, pathogenic microbes and their poisonous metabolic products. Scattered on the floor, it decreases the detrimental gas (ammonia) concentration of the air in the loft, and its humidity. Given internally, similarly to medical carbon, its effect is to decrease diarrhoea by adsorbing harmful substances.

One very important characteristic is that it is **very rich in trace and micro elements**. When it enters the system, zeolite deposits these elements, thus helping the metabolism and especially the operation of the **immune system**.

We add it to feed in a proportion of around 2-3%, but we can also offer it to the pigeons separately on trays. We can mix zeolite into drinking water if it is of a suitable form, which enriches the water with trace elements and stops pathogens from proliferating in it.

Zeolite is an entirely **natural substance**, and we do not have to prepare for side-effects. We only have to ensure that we do not administer it together with other drugs, as it can also block their active ingredients.

For all these reasons, it would be worth making greater and more widespread use of zeolite than we see in the world today.

(It is beyond the scope of this book, but we think it worth mentioning that zeolite also proves its worth in human medicine. It has repeatedly been shown that it is excellent for abolishing or greatly helping heartburn or gastralgia if administered internally, and sores and chronic ulceration of the limbs if given externally in powder form! It also binds and removes poisonous heavy metals – e.g. lead.)

3.b Performance boosters

L-carnitine

L-carnitine helps those materials (fatty acids) reach the heart from which the heart will principally gain its energy when operating. After filling the system with carnitine, the heart muscle withstands the burden more easily, and/or it is capable of displaying heightened performance over a longer period.

Carnitine also plays a key role in the operation of the skeletal muscles (pectoral muscles), increasing their performance. Just as in the case of heart muscles, it helps the regeneration of the skeletal musculature following strain, and shortens the period of regeneration.

It is recommended during the breeding season and before it, because it also has a good effect on the reproductive organs.

Its recommended dose is 0.1g per kilogram of body weight, for 1-2 days before races. If the treatment has a different objective (e.g. increasing fertility), we should administer for longer, but in partial doses.

Prolonged dosage of carnitine has a negative effect. If we administer it for three or more consecutive days in high doses, the body stops its production of carnitine, and it takes time before it can begin again. This can cause problems in races lasting for a number of days, when the artificially-administered carnitine runs out on the second day, and the pigeon's body is not able to restart its own production quickly enough. On such occasions the metabolism of the heart muscle and skeletal muscle becomes impaired, leading to a decline in flying performance or in severe cases to damage of the muscle cells.

Accordingly, we should be careful with the dosage of carnitine, and a treatment of three days before a race is the maximum. Experience suggests that treatment over two days is preferable, however; indeed, even a single application can bring visible results. There is a particularly strong increase in the performance of pigeons that have hitherto been flying less well.

As it is a doping substance, we can expect further negative effects of the artificial provision of carnitine. Through the heart muscle, carnitine compels the whole system to higher performance. But exaggerated performance results always carry the inherent risk of strain or injury. In theory, the pigeon's body is naturally "programmed" for the performance and tolerance capacity of the various organs to be in harmony. If we force one particular organ to overperform, we also overstrain the other organs. For this reason, if – staying with our example – the heart muscle is not damaged by the increased intake of carnitine, the heightened performance of the heart muscle forces the skeletal muscles, ligaments and joints to work harder and more intensively than usual, from which they can suffer damage that may be permanent.

Iodine

Iodine is an important constituent of the thyroid gland hormone, which plays a key role in metabolic processes, and a large role in the development of a perfect plumage. Thus an inadequate provision of iodine for racing pigeons causes a decline in flying performance for a number of reasons.

We should administer products containing iodine once or twice a week, but be careful when doing so, as it is easy to overdose it, particularly if we also use it to disinfect drinking water.

Carbohydrates

The body gains the energy necessary for muscle operation most easily and quickly from mono- and disaccharides. To help flying performance, we should usually give glucose, fructose or maltodextrin. Another natural source of energy is honey.

We should take care when administering carbohydrates, as an excessive amount can cause zymotic indigestion (dyspepsia), and thereby severe diarrhoea!

Iron

Iron plays a role in the production of haemoglobins, and thus in the transport of oxygen. We should give it to racing pigeons on a weekly basis for their blood to contain sufficient haemoglobins.

A number of illnesses can cause anaemia, e.g. intestinal worms, coccidiosis, lack of certain trace elements, and dicumarol poisoning. Alongside controlling the original illness, the necessary substitution of iron must also be ensured. If we suspect a lack of iron or anaemia, we should ask our veterinarian to conduct a blood test!

4. Antiparasitic drugs

Anti-coccidiosis drugs

amprolium

Amprolium has an effect on pathogens by inhibiting vitamin B1, but puts a burden on the pigeon's system for precisely the same reason. It causes dejection and tiredness.

Can be combined with ronidazole.

Dosage: 0.3 grams per litre of drinking water, for 5 days. In severe cases we should administer it again, in a half-dose, after a 2-day break.

Contraindication: We should not use it before races, fairs or pairing! We should not administer products containing vitamin B1 at the same time or directly afterwards!

sulfaclozine-Na

Has a broad spectrum, and is effective against many types of coccidia. It does not cause significant side-effects, but an overdose can cause haemophilia. On such occasions it may be necessary to give vitamin K.

Dosage: 0.5-0.6 grams per litre of drinking water, administered continuously over three days.
Can also be used intermittently, when it should be administered on the 1st, 2nd, 5th, 6th and 9th days.

Contraindication: Cannot be given in combination with monensin, narasin or salinomycin.

sulfadimethoxine-Na

Sulfadimethoxine combined with trimethoprim is effective against coccidia. Its advantage is that it is also effective against salmonella and coli, as well as staphylococci and haemophilus.

Dosage: 0.3-0.4 grams per litre of drinking water, over 3-4 days.

Contraindication: Cannot be given in the event of hepatic or renal dysfunction, nor that of reduced water consumption.

sulfaquinoxalin-Na

Sulfaquinoxalin combined with trimethoprim is effective against coccidia. Its advantage is that it is also effective against salmonella and coli.

Dosage: 0.25 grams per litre of drinking water, for 3-5 days. In severe cases we can repeat the treatment after a week's break.

Contraindication: Cannot be given in the event of reduced water consumption.

toltrazuril

A strong anti-coccidiosis drug, as it is effective against coccidia in many stages of their development. It is hardly absorbed from the gut, is not toxic to the system, and so can also be given in breeding and racing seasons.

It is primarily for therapeutic use, and should only be used for preventive treatment if this is deemed necessary. For instance, if in the last racing season we had our fair share of problems with coccidia, we should include it in our treatment schedule: after every fourth arrival home, we should conduct a two-day "preventive" cleansing treatment.

Thanks to its special characteristics, it is sufficient to administer toltrazuril for two days even for therapeutic treatment. If the infection was severe, we should repeat the course after five days.

Dosage: 0.025 grams per litre of drinking water for 2 days.

Deworming drugs

We administer deworming products in one go, usually every three months, or as often as every month during racing season. If after a course of treatment we see that worms have been released in the pigeons' faeces, it is advisable to repeat the treatment 2-3 weeks later. This is required because – contrary to popular belief – deworming drugs have no long-term effects, and in principle the pigeon can become reinfected with eggs still in its environment as early as the day after treatment.

On the day after any deworming process, we should conduct a spring clean in the loft to remove all the worms and worm eggs that have been released into the outside world.

Unlike coccidia, worm eggs must not be allowed to be present in droppings in any quantity. In the case of a positive laboratory result, we must immediately conduct a deworming course without fail.

abamectin

Member of the avermectin family. In pigeon-breeding it is a relatively new drug, but one whose popularity is spreading quickly. It should be dripped on the surface of the bird's skin. It is highly effective against hairworms and large roundworms, but has no effect on tapeworms. On the other hand, it is also effective against the majority of external parasites, and so by using it we (figuratively!) kill two birds with one stone. It is ideal for individual treatment.

When using it we should take care that the product reaches the skin directly, and not the feathers. For a few days before and after administering it, it is not advisable to bathe the birds, as the bathing water can decrease the product's effectiveness.

Dosage: 0.4-1.0 mg per kilogram of body weight, dripped onto the skin. In cases of severe infection we should repeat the treatment after two weeks.

fenbendazole

A drug with a broad spectrum, that is effective against hairworms, large roundworms and also tapeworms. Its further advantage is that it has an effect on adult worms, on transient larvae, and even on eggs.

Its disadvantage is that it is not water-soluble, and so has to be mixed with feed or ideally administered individually.

Dosage: 0.02 g per kilogram of body weight, administered once.

Contraindication: We should not give it to birds that are less than two months old, in the breeding season, or in the main moulting season.

ivermectin

Member of the avermectin family. It is effective against hairworms and large roundworms, as well as the majority of external parasites. It has no effect on tapeworms.

It can also be used by dripping onto the skin, but it is most commonly administered orally. Some use it in injection form, but in this case we must be prepared for strong irritation of and even damage to tissue!

Dosage: 1-1.5mg per kilogram of body weight, administered orally.

levamisole

Levamisole is one of the components of tetramisole. Its anthelmintic spectrum is similar to that of tetramisole, but is less toxic to the pigeon's system, and so is better recommended for treatment of the flock as a whole, although its price is far higher than that of the basic compound. It has immunostimulant properties.

Dosage: 0.025 grams per kilogram of body weight, administered orally. It can also be used as an injection, for which its dosage is 0.018-0.02 grams per kilogram.

Contraindication: It is contraindicated for weakened birds under heavy stress, especially in injection form. The latter should not be given in the event of kidney or liver insufficiency, either!

mebendazole

Has a broad spectrum, and is effective against hairworms, large roundworms and tapeworms. It also has an effect on the transient larvae forms.

It is normally brought to market in forms that are not soluble in water.

Dosage: 0.05 grams per kilogram of body weight, administered orally. It can be scattered on feed or applied individually.

moxidectin

A highly effective drug that provides prolonged protection against reinfestation; a member of the milbemycin family. It is effective against large round and hairworms, and against external parasites.

It is not so toxic and is safe to administer. It can be given during the pairing and moulting seasons, and neither is its use contraindicated between races.

Dosage: 1mg per kilogram of body weight, mixed into the drinking water. The calculated dosage must be spread across the whole of the day.

praziquantel

A pyrazine derivative which also has an effect on both adult and developing forms of tapeworm. It has no effect on eggs, however, and so thorough cleaning is required after deworming.

Dosage: 0.012-0.015 grams per kilogram of body weight.

tetramisole

Primarily effective against large roundworms and hairworms. The larvae are sensitive to it during all stages of their development.

It dissolves well in water, but is very bitter, and so pigeons are not keen on drinking it, and it can only be used for treating the flock if its members are made thirsty beforehand.

It is quite a toxic substance, but the birds are relatively tolerant to it. But even an overdose of twice the required amount can cause neurological symptoms, or the pigeons may regurgitate what they have consumed of it.

Dosage: 0.04 grams per kilogram of body weight, once the birds are made thirsty.

Medical herb extracts

These help prevent coccidiosis, canker and intestinal worms. In the case of severe infections or fully developed illnesses, however, their use is not adequate in and of itself. But they have the unquestionable advantage that they are natural materials, that are less of a burden on the pigeon's body and its environment. In addition, they are a valuable source of trace elements, and stimulate the appetite.

Dosage: We should generally use them twice a week throughout the year in the prescribed dosage. In the racing season, or in other stressful periods, it is recommended that they be used more than twice a week.

Drugs against external parasites

Depending on the base material, these products are applied onto the pigeon's body by dusting, spraying, soaking, or dripping them on the skin. When using them, we should avoid contact with the eyes and nasal or buccal cavities.

The following drugs have become prevalent in pigeon-breeding, and can be used safely:

- abamectin (dripped onto the skin)

- bioresmethrin
- chlorpyrifos
- chlor vinyl dimethyl phosphate
- fenoxycarb
- ivermectin (administered orally or dripped onto the skin)
- moxidectin (administered orally)
- permethrin
- pyrethrin
- tetrametrin
- transmix

Anti-canker drugs

Drugs used for canker vary significantly in their toxicity and their safety margin. Dimetridazole is the most toxic and thus has the narrowest safety margin; metronidazole and carnidazole are less dangerous, and ronidazole is the least toxic.

Not all products are available in all countries. And yet, if we are able to, we should alternate them regularly when using them, every six months or every year, to prevent or avoid resistance to them from developing. Our experience is that it is dimetridazole and metronidazole that lose their effectiveness most easily. This is probably because dimetridazole has been in widespread use for a long time, while metronidazole is unfortunately often only administered on a one-off basis (a quarter of one tablet given only once).

Immediately before and after pairing, and during rearing, we must use them with extreme care, as they can cause infertility, and, if released in greater quantities through the crop milk, can poison chicks. If we have no choice but to treat at such times, it is best not to choose dimetridazole, but rather the less toxic ronidazole, carnidazole or metronidazole. But we would do better to time the administering of these substances during incubation, if cleansing treatment did not take place before pairing.

carnidazole

Drug with a wide safety margin. It is one of the least toxic of the drugs for canker, and so it can be administered during the racing season, the moulting season, and in the breeding season (see above). It is usually only available in tablet form, and is thus time-consuming for treatment of the flock as a whole.

Dosage: 0.01g per pigeon, for at least three days, or until symptoms cease.

dimetridazole

One of the most toxic of the drugs used against canker. It is forbidden to use it in many countries. Where it is approved, we should take great care not to overdose it!

It dissolves well in water, and so is suitable – with the appropriate caution – for treating the whole flock.

Dosage: 0.5g per litre of drinking water. For preventive use, administer for three days, for healing treatment, for 4-6 days.

Warning! We always calculate the daily dosage on the basis of an **average** day's consumption of drinking water! If water consumption rises because of hot weather or for other reasons, the increase should **NOT** be followed by an increase in the daily dose!

metronidazole

Moderately toxic. In its pure form, it is insoluble in water, but it can be suspended in an aqueous solution. In this form it is also suitable for treating the flock as a whole, but the pigeons are not usually keen on drinking the solution because of its taste. In tablet form it is very suitable for treatment on an individual basis.

Dosage: 0.05-0.06g per pigeon, depending on body weight or the severity of the disease, for at least three days.

ronidazole

The least toxic substance in its group. Its period of treatment is also shorter than the average. If we have to treat during pairing, we should choose ronidazole. We can also use it during the racing and moulting seasons.

It can be combined with amprolium, thus producing a medication that is effective against coccidiosis. We should not use this combination during the racing seasons, however.

Dosage: 0.2g per litre of drinking water for 2-3 days.

5. Antifungal drugs

Fungal diseases are only rarely diagnosed in pigeons, and accordingly the range of veterinary products available for internal use is modest, to say the least. It is more likely that we can use one of the products used in human healthcare, if this is needed.

Yeast

Yeast fungi, which do not otherwise cause illness, can overproliferate (primarily in the crop) if the body's immune system is pathologically weakened. Another eventuality is that they proliferate overly while under the "protection" of antibiotic treatment.

If necessary, the fungal proliferation can be restrained by administering **nystatin**. Its dosage is 50,000 – 100,000 units per pigeon, once a day. Once symptoms disappear, the treatment still needs to be continued for another three days!

Repeated appearance of the illness is a sign of severe weakness of the immune system, and such pigeons should be removed.

Aspergillosis

As we mentioned in the corresponding section, in the event of advanced aspergillosis that has spread, recovery is essentially hopeless, and treatment is lengthy and expensive, and so we advise the removal of the ill pigeon. In less severe instances, we can choose from the following active ingredients:

itraconazole

Dosage: 10mg per kilogram of body weight, administered orally, once daily, over a period of 3-6 weeks!

ketoconazole

Dosage: 30mg per kilogram of body weight, administered orally, once daily, over a period of 3-6 weeks!

6. Vaccines

The use of vaccinations is intended to provide individual specimens and the whole flock with protection against the disease in question. Because of its importance, we will repeat again here that with the threat of circovirus infection, individual vaccinations must be administered at the youngest possible age.

Nowadays it is impossible to imagine economic and successful pigeon-breeding anywhere in the world without regular use of vaccinations. In addition, active protection against paramyxovirus is obligatory in most countries.

The vaccines used in pigeon-breeding usually protect against one particular pathogen, and so we refer to them as monovalent vaccines. Vaccines that are effective against two pathogens at once we call bivalent, and we can also find examples of this in pigeon care. Vaccines that contain more than two active ingredients are called polyvalent, but in pigeon-breeding these are not common.

Monovalent vaccines

Vaccines against paramyxovirus

It is with regard to vaccines used against diseases caused by paramyxovirus that demand is best satisfied. (Indeed, sometimes almost too well, leading to a competitive battle between pharmaceutical companies producing the various vaccines – which often try to influence even local pigeon associations.) There are products available specifically approved for pigeons, but many also use the vaccines produced against Newcastle disease (avian pneumoencephalitis) in chickens. The latter are usually injections, but are also distributed in a form that can be administered orally.

Vaccines containing the Newcastle disease (avian pneumoencephalitis) virus

These vaccines do not contain pigeon PMV, but its "parent" virus, the original Newcastle disease virus (most commonly the so-called La Sota strain). Their use is very widespread, despite the fact that products specifically made for pigeon PMV are also available. Their prevalence is partly thanks to their relatively low price, and partly to the fact that previously, before the appearance of specific pigeon PMV vaccines, these represented the only defence against the virus.

As the Newcastle disease (NCD) virus is only related (albeit closely) to pigeon PMV, in pigeons the capacity of such vaccines to provide immunity does not in principle reach that of PMV-specific vaccines. (This is particularly true of vaccines used in drinking water.) Still, the majority of these vaccines gives good protection, and thus their use with adequate regularity provides sufficient immunity against pigeon PMV. This can be stated with confidence, based on pigeon fanciers' experience over many years, all the more so because in recent years vaccines containing the original Newcastle disease virus (e.g. the La Sota strain) have appeared and gained approval for use with pigeons.

The earliest possible time for their use varies, but some can already be administered at the age of three weeks.

Vaccines containing pigeon-specific paramyxovirus

These vaccines actually contain the pigeon PMV that causes the illness in pigeons. So, assuming they are used professionally, it is from them that we can expect the highest level and longest duration of protection. According to their official description, the earliest they can usually be used is when birds are five weeks old.

Note

Protection against pigeon PMV is obligatory in many countries. Which vaccine is officially accepted, however, varies from country to country, and such regulations are known to change. Before applying the vaccination, we should ask about the current requirements, if we do not want to encounter unpleasant surprises at races and fairs.

Many fanciers follow the practice of alternating the virus strain of the vaccine used. First they administer the vaccine against Newcastle disease, often choosing one that is added to drinking water. Two or three weeks later they use the vaccine specific to pigeon PMV. Our experience suggests that this is a good technique which results in a high level of protection.

Vaccines used against pox virus

When using a vaccine against pox we should take great care to immunize every member of the flock at the same time. It can be given from the age of five weeks, and an annual booster injection is recommended. As the virus survives in the environment for a long time, specimens in a yard that has once been infected should be given systematic vaccinations for at least 8-10 years afterwards.

Some products should be used in a different way from the other vaccines, by rubbing them into the feather follicules. (This is described in detail in the section on pigeon pox).

Anti-paratyphoid vaccines

These vaccines generally contain the strain Salmonella typhimurium var. Copenhagen. Sadly, although demand for them would be high, in many countries anti-typhoid products are only accessible with great difficulty, if at all.

There are vaccines that contain killed or weakened salmonella bacteria, with their inherent benefits and disadvantages.

Vaccines containing killed pathogens

Advantages

Put less of a burden on the flock. If absolutely necessary, they can be used to vaccinate a flock already displaying symptoms, and their effect is not ruined by an antibiotic administered at the same time.

Disadvantages

Elicit a rather weaker immunization result, and the protection they offer is weaker and lasts for a shorter time. At least three vaccinations are required in the first year, which then have to be repeated every six months.

Vaccines containing live, attenuated pathogens

Advantages

Provide a higher level of protection. A single shot can provide adequate protection, and it is enough to repeat them every 9-12 months.

Disadvantages

They put a greater burden on the flock, and induce more unwanted reactions after the vaccination. **Antibiotics must not be used** within five days before and after the vaccination. If this does prove necessary, we can expect the vaccination to lose some of its effectiveness, so it is advisable to give a booster shot to such specimens a few weeks later.

In general, anti-paratyphoid vaccines can be given from the age of 4-6 weeks.

Note

It is worth noting – especially given the difficulty of acquiring them – that customized, so-called flock vaccines against paratyphoid can be ordered from veterinary laboratories specialising in this. After a sample is taken, the strains currently present in the flock are cultured artificially, and a vaccine is produced from this bacterial culture. One great advantage of such vaccines is that they defend precisely against the strain causing the problem in the given pigeon flock, and so allow us to achieve the highest possible level of effectiveness. Their disadvantage is that they are more expensive than mass-produced vaccines, and their preparation takes time.

Bivalent vaccines

By using bivalent vaccines we can save precious time, for two reasons. Firstly, we only have to perform one vaccination instead of two, which itself is time-saving, and also means that the flock is only burdened half as much. Secondly, we can save a week or two in developing protection against illnesses, which bearing in mind the circovirus threat to chicks is far from being an insignificant consideration.

In pigeon care we typically find bivalent vaccines that protect against paramyxovirus and pox virus. We can generally use these for the first time at around the age of 5-6 weeks.

Polyvalent vaccines

Polyvalent vaccines are widely available in dog and cat care, for example, but not yet common for pigeons. Polyvalent pigeon vaccines are at the testing stage in some countries, but research into their effectiveness and their official registration are tasks for the future.

Over a number of years I had the opportunity to try out a certain polyvalent vaccine, which contained five different agents (against paramyxovirus, paratyphoid, herpes, mycoplasma and chlamydia). Everyday experience showed that the vaccine provided adequate protection against all five diseases, if it was administered three times in the first year of life. (When the pigeon was three weeks old, then 6-8 weeks, then about six months.) Afterwards the birds vaccinated three times in their first year had to be vaccinated once a year. It was when we vaccinated older birds that had not received the same vaccine when young that we saw unquestionably negative reactions appear (languishment, dejection, possibly more severe symptoms, even death). These negative side-effects were not observed with specimens vaccinated from a young age, and these birds acquired a long-lasting high level of immunity against all five diseases.

When discussing polyvalent vaccines, we should add that in theory these vaccines have disadvantages. Firstly, the level of resistance that develops to each illness is lower, because after the multi-component vaccine is administered the energies and attention of the body's immune system are divided. This can be compensated for by using the polyvalent vaccines three or even four times in the first year of the pigeon's life.

Another disadvantage is that a polyvalent vaccine causes a larger burden for the body all at once than a monovalent one, and so can only be given to a flock in a fine state of health, and even then we can expect negative reactions in the days after the vaccination. This is particularly true if the polyvalent vaccine contains bacterial agents.

Note

It is generally true of all vaccines that if at all possible, we should immunize the entire flock, or at least all specimens in a particular loft, at once. Another golden rule is that the vaccinations should be completed at the very least 3-4 weeks before the pairing or racing season. If administered close to the breeding season, the vaccination can make eggs infertile, while during racing season it can lead to a decline in performance, or be dangerous because of the **negative phase**.

Negative phase

For 2-3 weeks after vaccination, we must be particularly careful that the vaccinated birds not be exposed to any kind of source of infection. For this is when they pass through the so-called **negative phase**, during which their system is highly sensitive to infection. The essence of the negative phase is that the inoculated virus or bacterium immediately neutralizes some of the antibodies present from maternal origin or from an earlier vaccination, and it is only 10-14 days later that the vaccine induces a level of immunity higher than the initial one. That is to say, **for about two weeks after the vaccination is given, there will be less protective material in the system than there was previously!**

Finally, it is very useful if we raise the active protection of our pigeons to the highest possible level in the first year of their lives with booster shots.

7. Disinfectants

We use disinfectants to destroy or reduce the number of microorganisms hiding in the outside world, on the walls, floor and furnishings of the loft, by either washing, spraying or vaporizing. These microorganisms are bacteria, viruses, fungi, and their spores, if they have any, as well as coccidia and the various stages of parasites, eggs and larvae. When using disinfectants we should bear the following in mind:

- If possible, we should use modern disinfectant products that have a broad antimicrobial effect.

- If we want to disinfect to protect against a particular pathogen, we should make sure that the product we wish to use is suitable for destroying the given pathogen. Not all disinfectants destroy all kinds of bacterium or virus.

- The disinfection should always be preceded by thorough cleaning! The disinfectant does not reach the pathogens hiding in remaining dirt in adequate concentration. The effective disinfection of a clean loft requires significantly less disinfectant, which is both economical and environmentally-conscious.

- We must not mix up the various disinfectants! The commercially available products are powerful enough on their own. Mixing them can lead to a reduction in effectiveness, and even to accidents (generating harmful, possibly explosive gases)!

- We should follow the manufacturers' instructions when diluting a product! Within the given range it is usually advisable to make the solution as concentrated as possible, but we should not go outside this range. It is also important for the disinfectant to have time to take effect. This takes at least ten to fifteen minutes, but it is better if we leave the agent on the given surface for even longer.

- Pigeons must not come into contact with the majority of disinfectants or their fumes, as most of their chemically active ingredients will cause damage to their health!

- We should use the recommended protective materials! This certainly means rubber gloves, and when spraying or vaporizing the product, especially in a closed space, we definitely need equipment to protect our breathing, as well. In fact, in a closed space even a simple washing down with the product can lead to the accumulation of harmful gases and vapours in concentrations that could damage one's health.

- When storing and using disinfectants, we should take great care that there is no chance that children might come in contact with them!

- Should disinfectants accidentally be swallowed or get into the eyes, we should consult a doctor immediately, and in the latter case rinse the eye repeatedly with clean water in the meantime! We should also stop working with the disinfectant and consult a doctor if we feel at all unwell or faint!

- The disinfectant and its packaging are also hazardous for the environment.
- Circovirus is a particularly resistant virus, and so we should take particular care when disinfecting to get rid of it!

*

Lime

Whitewashing with lime is an obsolete technique in pigeon-breeding. Lime that is spread on the wall only has adequate disinfecting properties until it dries, after which it loses its effectiveness. Indeed, by making the environment slightly alkaline it is expressly favourable for salmonella and coli strains.

Halogen elements

Iodine is a safe disinfectant if its concentration in the solution reaches 1%. It destroys all pathogens, bacteria, fungi and viruses. We can also expect good results from compounds containing **active chlorine** (e.g. bleach). The latter in particular produce poisonous gases, and can also ruin other disinfectants and their effect, and so we should be circumspect when using them!

Of compounds containing chlorine, we should give preference to those which are not bound in alkaline compounds, and one or two days after their use we should wash or spray the loft with a lightly acidic substance (diluted apple vinegar), thereby turning the surroundings from alkaline to acidic.

Chlorine-cresol

Thanks to their thick shells, parasite eggs are highly resistant, and so general antimicrobial disinfectants do not have sufficient effect on them. Chlorine-cresol is specifically suitable for the destruction of coccidia and various forms of intestinal worms in the outside world. It is also effective against trichomonads, as well as viruses and fungi. Protective materials must be worn when using it!

Organic acids

Undiluted organic acids have adequate disinfecting powers in and of themselves, but they are dangerous and highly corrosive, and so must not be used in undiluted form. They perform a fine service when diluted, however. The use of **apple vinegar** is the most highly recommended, which as a natural substance is not in the right concentration harmful to pigeons or to their environment; indeed, if it enters the pigeons' bodies it is an important source of organic acids and trace elements. To disinfect drinking water we should put a full teaspoon of 5% apple vinegar into every litre of water. We use a slightly more concentrated solution to clean the cage, but if we sense a pungent smell, we should not forget to ventilate.

Essential oils

Essential oils are not only useful for treating pigeons, but also for disinfecting the loft. We generally find them in products that we use, in spray form, to disinfect the air. They can be a help in preventing or curing respiratory diseases, but we should be careful when using these oils, because they can irritate the air passages if used in too high a concentration or for too long a period, and initiate inflammation in them.

Synthetic disinfectants

These are generally reliable disinfectants with an all-round effect in the battle against bacteria, viruses and fungi. Like most products, we should only use them in an empty loft, and use protective materials. They are very responsive to dirt left behind after inadequate cleaning. Their disadvantage is that they represent a heavy burden on their environment.

V. Treatment schedule

Many specialized articles and monographs recommend various types of treatment schedule, which when implemented for a particular flock may or may not be successful. The schedule is more likely to be effective if the writer of the article and the breeder taking his advice are not far from one another in terms of geography, climate, epidemiology, and, last but not least, financial resources. If they are very different in these respects, its success will be more muted. It is certain that there is no one schedule of treatment that can be used for all flocks; the discovery of such a schedule can be expected at about the same time as that of the perpetuum mobile.

In this book we do not put together any actual treatment schedules. Rather, we summarize the considerations that must be borne in mind by all breeders when they create **their own treatment schedule tailored to their own flock**. We hope that the reader of this book has already learned much useful information that may be of help in completing a task that is not at all easy and that requires very careful attention.

General considerations

- it is vital to **keep a diary of the flock** in order to prepare, implement and check the treatment schedule, and to learn lesson for future reference

- the first task is **precisely and objectively to determine the number of spaces** at our disposal

- the treatment schedule should be constructed around these **three periods**:
    - breeding
    - races

- moulting

- antibiotic treatments (even if preventive!) should always last **for at least three days**

- after antibiotics we should always give **probiotics** for 4-5 days

- young pigeons should always receive the necessary **vaccinations as early as possible**

- **immune boosters** given together with vaccinations raise the level of protection provided by the vaccine, and extend its period of effectiveness

- we should administer vitamins containing **selenium**, and probiotics, once or twice a week throughout the year

- a limited presence of **coccidia** in faeces is normal. Preventive treatment is justified if coccidiosis has manifested itself in the flock in the last year

- if there has been **pox** in the yard in the last ten years, we should not fail to plan a vaccination against pox virus

- if there is **intestinal worm** infection in the loft, we should plan a deworming treatment at flock level every 1-2 months over the next six to twelve months, and conduct lab tests at least this often

- we should always make a definite treatment schedule for the **quarantine**, paying special attention to the pigeons' vaccination histories

- it is useful if we can determine the exact times of sales and purchases, and thereby **changes to flock size**, in advance, for these influence the treatment schedule significantly

Particular considerations

Around the time of the breeding season

- the **vaccinations** are timed such that they finish at least four, but ideally more, weeks before pairing takes place

- about a month before pairing, we should **deworm** every specimen, for both external and internal worms

- beginning 20 days before pairing, for 10 days, antibiotic treatment against **salmonella**, ideally targeted and with an antibiotic that is not absorbed, if possible one that is less damaging for the normal intestinal bacteria

- against **trichomonads**, a treatment of 4-6 days is required, before pairing; on such occasions we should avoid using dimetridazole, as it can cause infertility

- if the treatment against canker did not take place prior to the pairing season, it is best to make up for it after the eggs are laid, during incubation

- before and during the breeding season, all the stock birds should be carefully supplied with vitamins, especially **vitamin E and carotene** (!), with macro elements, trace elements, especially selenium, and with immune boosters; the high level of immunity thus achieved, passed on through the egg, also protects youngsters in their first stage of life!

- towards the end of the rearing season, a targeted course of antibiotics for 6-8 days to prevent a re-emergence of **paratyphoid**, which is common at this time

Around the time of the racing season

- **deworming** before the racing season, and at the end of it, on one occasion each time

- treatment against **trichomonads** also takes place on one occasion before the season, and one after it, this time for 3-6 days (depending on the product used). It is possible to treat the bird for canker during the season, but this should also happen continuously for 3-4 days in a row, depending on the substance used. We begin this treatment on the day after the bird's arrival.

- if there is any need for **antibiotic treatment**, this should last for at least three days, even in the racing season. We should avoid the use of antibiotics, which put too much of a burden on the body (decline in performance). We begin the treatment on the day after the birds arrive.

- we should **not administer amprolium** during the racing season

- we should be careful with the dosage of **L-carnitine**, as an overdose causes a retrograde result. We should give carnitine for one day, or at most two, just before the races.

- every time the birds **come home** we should immediately give them a mineral mixture, vitamins, probiotics and an amino acid product that speeds the regeneration of muscles and other organs

- because infections are inevitable, during the whole racing season we should keep the defence systems of all pigeons at a high level (including those that stay at home!) giving them natural **immunostimulants**, that is herbal extracts, twice a week, and if necessary, artificial immune boosters as well

- many fanciers observe the custom of including one preventive treatment each week, alternating between bacteria, trichomonads, intestinal worms and coccidia, i.e. performing each of these every four weeks. It is not sure that the automatic, routine use of this procedure achieves the desired objective, i.e. of preventing diseases from appearing in the loft. It is better to decide the weighting given to the various treatments on the basis of the experience of the preceding years and that of the current racing season itself. If we had a lot of problems with canker last year, for example, but there was no coccidiosis, this year we can treat against canker every two or three weeks instead of treatment against coccidiosis. We would do even better to have **frequent laboratory tests** done during the racing season, primarily from faeces, and use the results to determine treatment.

Around the moulting season

- both before and after the moulting season we should plan a "**spring clean**" involving disinfection

- if possible, we should also plan the changing of the earth in the loft or the aviary, or in the case of a concrete **floor** its soaking with disinfectant, for this period

- it is advisable to begin **annual booster vaccinations** (paratyphoid, paramyxovirus) after the moulting season

- as development of new plumage requires a large amount of **iodine**, we should ensure that there is adequate provision of it. We should be careful when so doing, however, as too great an intake of iodine, vitamins and amino acids can be as damaging for moulting as their insufficiency.

Finally, we should not forget that in unforeseen circumstances – like the appearance of an illness, or the threat of an epidemic – **even the best of treatment schedules may have to be modified**.

VI. Glossary

We have endeavoured to include as few specialist terms in the book as possible. This glossary explains the terms that are used.

acute
develops suddenly, usually displays severe symptoms, short-lived (disease)

adsorb
to bind; some substance attaches some other substance to its surface

anthelmintic
medicine that is active against worms

avian pneumoencephalitis
Newcastle disease; a severe viral infectious disease in poultry with a high death toll

bactericidal
killer of bacteria

bacteriostatic
substance that prevents bacteria from proliferating further but does not kill them

blood level
the concentration of a given substance in the specimen's blood

booster shot
reminder vaccination; most vaccines require repeated injections to achieve and maintain an appropriate level of immunity. The first injection is called the "primary vaccination", followed by booster shots

chronic
when (e.g. a disease) is prolonged, present for a longer period

congenital
present at birth

dystrophy

degeneration of a certain tissue or organ

enterococci
here: a group of beneficial intestinal bacteria needed for normal digestion in animals and humans

hepatic
of or pertaining to the liver

hepatoprotective
helps the functioning of the liver and/or a material that protects the cells of the liver

immune booster
a substance that strengthens the immune system

immunostimulant
a substance that strengthens the immune system

lactobacilli
a group of beneficial intestinal bacteria needed for normal digestion in animals and humans. They are typically present in yogurt and kefir

multiresistant
here: a strain of bacteria that is resistant to the majority of antibiotics

osteomalacia
softening of the bones in adults; decalcification

OTC or **over-the-counter**
product that can be acquired without a veterinarian's prescription

probiotic
product containing useful intestinal bacteria capable of proliferation

protein anabolism

the body's own production of proteins from amino acids

renal
of or pertaining to the kidneys

safety margin
the range of dosage within which the drug takes effect without representing a threat to the system – the narrower the margin, the higher the risk of overdose

susceptibility test
an *in vitro* test to determine a particular bacterium strain's susceptibility (or resistance) to an array of antibiotics

systemic
of or pertaining to the body or system as a whole

therapeutic spectrum
for antibiotics: the wider the therapeutic spectrum, the more species of bacteria the medicine is effective against

toxicosis
disease produced by a toxin, poisoning

vector
an ectoparasite (usually an arthropod, e.g. a tick or a mosquito) that transmits diseases by passing pathogenic microorganisms on to animals and/or humans

VII. Bibliography

Adenovirus
(Gordon A. Chalmers, D.V.M., Internet article)

Bacterial Infections of the Intestines of Pigeons

(Gordon A. Chalmers, D.V.M., Internet article)

Canker in Racing Pigeons
(J.F. Higgins, V.M.D., Internet article)

Circovirus
(Gordon A. Chalmers, D.V.M., Internet article)

E. coli & Racing Pigeons
(Cathy Hooper, D.V.M., Internet article)

Health Program for Racing Pigeons
(Cathy Hooper, D.V.M., Internet article)

Infectious diseases of domestic animals *(A háziállatok fertőző betegségei)*
(Dr. Tamás Szent-Iványi – Dr. János Mészáros, 1985)

Nutrition and the Fuels for Flight
(G. A. Chalmers, D.V.M., Internet article)

Pigeon Diseases *(Tauben-krankheiten)*
(Dr. Werner Lüthgen, 1994.)

Pigeon questions & answers
(Peter Pobor, Sacramento USA, Internet article)

Poultry Hygiene *(Baromfi-egészségtan)*
(Dr. János Mészáros, Ed., 1976)

Respiratory aspergillosis in wild and domestic birds *(Légzőszervi aspergillosis vad- és díszmadarakban)*
(Dr. Gabriella Vissi, Dr. György Barátossy, Kisállatpraxis, 2002)

Selected Diseases of Racing Pigeons
(Gordon A. Chalmers, D.V.M., Internet article)

The Flying Vet`s Pigeon Health Management
(Dr. Colin Walker, 2000)

The Health of Pigeons *(Gesunde tauben)*
(Ludwig Schrag, 2000)

Veterinary Epidemiology I (*Állatorvosi járványtan I.)*
(Dr. Tuboly Sándor, Ed., 1998)

Veterinary Epidemiology II *(Állatorvosi járványtan II.)*
(Dr. János Varga, Ed., 1999)

Veterinary Pharmacology *(Állatorvosi gyógyszertan)*
(Dr. Gábor Semjén – Dr. Péter Laczay)

Veterinary products 2002 *(Állatgyógyászati készítmények 2002)*
(Dr. János Perényi, Ed.)

Tables

Table 1. Conversion tables

Table 2. Comparison of the symptoms of contagious diseases Young age group

Table 3. Comparison of the symptoms of contagious diseases Older age group

Table 4. Therapeutic spectrum of antibiotics

The table shows the effect various types of antibiotics theoretically have on different species of bacteria, and which bacteria they never have an effect on. It also shows what, according to our experience, the level of resistance is.

(The antibiotics *in italics* are those that are not absorbed adequately from the intestine, if at all.)

Table 5. The damaging effect of antibiotics on normal flora

Table 1. Conversion Tables

WEIGHTS:

1 pound (lb) = 0.454 kg = 454 grams

1 kilogram (kg) = 2.2 pounds = 1000 grams

1 gram = 1000 mg

LIQUID MEASURE:

1 gallon (gal.) US = 3.785 liters = 3785 ml

1 gallon (gal.) UK = 4.54 liters = 4540 ml

1 tablespoon = 15 ml = 3 teaspoons

1 teaspoon = 5 ml

1 liter = 1000 ml

1 deciliter (dl) = 100 ml

1 milliliter (ml) = 1 cubic centimeter (cc)

TEMPERATURE CONVERSION:

°F = (°C x 1.8) + 32

°C = (°F - 32) x .555 = °C

Note

As teaspoons are not produced according to a universal standard, and different powders do not always of the same density, administering medicines by spoon is not a very reliable method. We do best to acquire a simple gram scale and measure out the dose accurately. (The cost of the scale is soon recouped from the savings made by avoiding wastage of medicine or damage from underdoses and overdoses.)

It is best to measure out products in liquid form with plastic syringes of the appropriate size.

Table 2. Comparison of the symptoms of contagious diseases Young age group

	diarrhoea	neurological symptom	sudden death	nasal discharge	skin alterations	respiratory symptoms	weight loss	lack of appetite	abnormal plumage	alterations to joints	typical symptom
paratyphoid	■	○	■	—	—	○	■	■	—	○	sudden death
paramyxovirus	■	●	●	—	—	—	●	○	■	—	pseudo-diarrhoea
trichomonas	●	—	●	—	—	○	●	●	—	—	yellowish nodules; diarrhoea
coli	●	—	●	○	—	●	●	●	—	○	death of egg; blood poisoning
adenovirus	■	—	■	—	—	—	○	○	—	—	full crop
circovirus	■	○	●	●	○	●	●	●	■	○	many different symptoms within the loft
mycoplasma	○	—	○	■	—	■	○	○	—	—	conjunctivitis
chlamydia	■	—	○	■	—	■	●	■	—	—	green diarrhoea; one eye affected
pox	○	—	○	○	■	○	●	●	—	—	clinging crusts
herpes	●	○	○	■	—	■	●	●	■	—	from the age of 2 to 6 months
haemophilus	○	—	—	■	—	■	—	■	—	—	spreads quickly
coccidiosis	■	—	○	—	—	—	●	■	—	—	brownish, sanguineous droppings
intestinal worms	●	○	—	—	—	—	■	■	■	—	weight loss
fungal toxins	●	○	●	○	—	○	●	■	—	—	poisoning symptoms
aspergillosis	○	○	○	●	—	●	●	●	—	○	hard, clinging button

■ common symptom, present in most cases ○ uncommon symptom
● common symptom, but often not present — no such symptom

Table 3. Comparison of the symptoms of contagious diseases Older age group

	diarrhoea	neurological symptom	sudden death	nasal discharge	skin alterations	respiratory symptoms	weight loss	lack of appetite	abnormal plumage	alterations to joints	typical symptom
paratyphoid	●	○	○	—	—	○	○	●	●	■	swelling of joints
paramyxovirus	■	■	○	—	—	—	●	○	—	—	neurological symptoms
trichomonas	○	—	—	—	—	●	○	○	—	—	reduced performance
coli	●	—	○	○	—	●	○	○	●	○	chronic organ inflammations
adenovirus	●	—	■	—	—	—	—	■	—	—	sudden death
circovirus											(reduced performance)
mycoplasma	○	—	○	■	—	■	○	○	—	—	conjunctivitis_
chlamydia	■	—	○	■	—	■	●	■	—	—	green diarrhoea; one eye affected
pox											(reduced performance)
herpes											(reduced performance)
haemophylus	○	—	—	■	—	■	—	■	—	—	upper respiratory organs
coccidiosis	■	—	—	—	—	—	●	■	—	—	brownish, sanguineous droppings
intestinal worms	●	○	—	—	—	—	■	■	—	—	emaciation
fungal toxins	●	○	●	○	—	○	●	■	■	—	poisoning symptoms
aspergillosis	○	○	○	●	—	●	●	●	—	○	hard, clinging nodule

■ common symptom, present in most cases ○ uncommon symptom
● common symptom, but often not present — no such symptom

Table 4. Therapeutic spectrum of antibiotics

	salmo -nella	E. coli	myco- plasma	chla- mydia	haemo -philus	pyog. cocci
amoxicillin	●	●	—	—	■	●
amoxic. + clav. acid	■	■	—	—	■	■
ampicillin	●	●	—	—	●	●
colistin	■	■				
cephalosporin	○	○	—	—	○	■
chlortetracycline	●	●	■	■		●
difloxacin	●	●	■	●	●	
doxycycline	○	○	■	■	■	●
enrofloxacin	■	■	■		■	●
erythromycin	—	—	■	○	■	●
furazolidone	●	●				
gentamycin	■	■			○	○
lincomycin	—	—	■			■
norfloxacin	■	■	■		■	●
oxytetracycline	○	○	■	●		●
spectinomycin	■	■	■			
streptomycin	●	○			■	●
sulfachlorpyridazine	●	●	■		●	●
tiamulin	—	—	■			○
tilozin	—	—	■			●

■ suitable in principle, and resistance to it is rare
● suitable in principle, but resistance to it is already common
○ would be suitable in principle, but resistance to it is very common
— unsuitable, even in principle

Table 5. The damaging effect of different antibiotics on pigeon normal intestinal flora, and on the microorganisms of commercially available probiotics, and yogurts

	normal intestinal bacteria pigeon 1	normal intestinal bacteria pigeon 2	commer-cial probiotic 1	commer-cial probiotic 2	commer-cial probiotic 3	natural yogurt	Cauca-sian yogurt (kefir)
amoxicillin	■	●	—	●	○	—	●
amoxic. + clav.	■	■	●	●	■	●	●
ampicillin	○	●	—	—	●	—	—
cephalosporin	—	○	—	—	○	—	—
colistin	●	■	■	■	—	■	○
difloxacin	■	●	■	■	●	■	○
doxycyclin	○	●	○	○	●	—	○
enrofloxacin	●	●	■	■	○	■	—
erythromycin	—	○	—	—	—	—	—
gentamycin	■	■	■	●	●	●	■
lincomycin	○	—	—	—	●	—	—
norfloxacin	●	■	●	●	○	●	○
oxytetracycline	●	●	○	●	■	—	○
penicillin	—	—	—	—	—	—	—
spectinomycin	—	○	—	—	—	—	—
streptomycin	○	—	—	—	—	—	—
sulfadimetoxine	●	○	○	●	●	●	—

■ strong damaging effect
● middling damaging effect
○ weakly damaging effect
— no, or insignificant damaging effect

Made in the USA
Coppell, TX
15 June 2023

18127329R00131